Scottish Highlanders

Scottish HIGHLANDERS

A PEOPLE AND THEIR PLACE

JAMES HUNTER

MAINSTREAM
PUBLISHING

EDINBURGH AND LONDON

Copyright © James Hunter, 1992
Photographs © Cailean Maclean

The moral right of the author has been asserted

First published in Great Britain 1992 by
MAINSTREAM PUBLISHING COMPANY (EDINBURGH) LTD
7 Albany Street
Edinburgh EH1 3UG

ISBN 1 85158 443 9 (cloth)

A catalogue record for this book is available from the British Library

Typeset in 12 /14pt Goudy Old Style by Combined Arts, Edinburgh
Printed in Great Britain by Butler & Tanner Ltd, Frome

*For
my mother
and
in memory of
my father*

ACKNOWLEDGMENTS

This is not a history book, but it deals quite a lot with history. In trying to elucidate what it is that makes the Scottish Highlands a very special place, I have relied heavily, therefore, on the findings of the various professional historians whose books are mentioned in my suggestions for further reading.

While undertaking the travels I made in connection with what follows, I incurred many other obligations. I am indebted, in particular, to the many people, most of whom are mentioned individually on subsequent pages, who dealt so patiently and helpfully with my questions and inquiries; in the United States, in Canada, in Ireland, Iona, Morvern, Ardnamurchan, Edinburgh, Islay, Aberdeenshire, Skye, Spean Bridge, Glen Roy, Inverness, Duror, Strathnaver, Bettyhill, South Uist, Benbecula, North Uist, Harris, Lewis and elsewhere.

That one-man compendium of Hebridean genealogy, Bill Lawson, made clear much of what would otherwise have remained obscure about my own Scottish Highland origins. And the nature of my personal links with Morvern, Strontian, Tiree and the Uists was further explained by my mother, Jean Hunter, my aunt, Mary McLachlan, and my other relatives, Donald Lawrie and John Bannerman.

John Bannerman, however, provided me with a great deal more than information about our mutual connections with Uist. But for the researches and writings of this Edinburgh University historian, the early history of Scotland, and especially of Gaelic Scotland, would be much less accessible than it now is to casual investigators like myself. And, but for John's kindness in

7

carefully reading and commenting upon a typescript version of this book, much questionable material would have appeared in several of the ensuing chapters. The responsibility for all such errors of fact and interpretation as may remain, I should make clear at this point, is entirely my own.

Bill Campbell, Peter MacKenzie and their colleagues at Mainstream encouraged the project from the outset and helped ensure that it kept, more or less, to schedule. Very welcome assistance with my research and travel costs was provided by a Glenfiddich Living Scotland Award. Cailean Maclean, a good friend as well as a colleague, made it possible for the book to be amply – and, in my opinion, very appropriately and expertly – illustrated. My wife, Evelyn, and our children, Iain and Anna, were, as they have always been, unstintingly supportive.

CHAPTER ONE

The evening's fifteenth piper has taken the stage and is energetically bouncing his music off palely painted brick walls decorated with garish posters advertising the merits of Budweiser and Miller beers. The clock above the bar is showing a few minutes short of midnight. Outside, where the temperature has been snuggling up to the hundred-degree mark for more than a week now, lightning glimmers sporadically. Thunder can be heard among the mountains. The rising wind, blowing through an open door behind me, smells of dried grass and sun-scorched pine trees.

This side of that door, where the air-conditioning system has long since yielded to the challenge posed by a crowd so thickly packed that shelves and window ledges are doubling as seats, Bruce Gandy, a carpenter by profession but a musician by inclination, is emerging as the clear winner of what the compère has enthusiastically assured us is the world famous jig and hornpipe contest held each year in the Fort Ground Tavern, 705 River Avenue, Coeur d'Alene, North Idaho.

The Highland bagpipe is taken very seriously here, and Bruce Gandy is clearly a master of it. But this evening is one when pipers participating in the local college's Scottish Studies Program are encouraged to relax a little. That is why Bruce, who plays regularly with the Fraser Highlanders in Toronto, is performing in a steeply plunging, one-piece swimsuit of a type that might conceivably be described as sensual if it did not clash just slightly with his beard.

We are, in every sense, a long, long way from Scotland. They do things differently here. But for all that pipers got up as drag artists and television cartoon characters – of whom there have been several gracing the Fort Ground Tavern stage this hot and sticky evening – would be most unlikely to appeal to the organisers of our more prosaic cultural festivals back home, this North American celebration of the Scottish Highlands is by no means simply frivolous.

Coeur d'Alene, a neat but bustling lakeside city now emerging as one of the USA's premier holiday resorts, is not, after all, the sort of place where the obvious way of putting in your days – especially at the height of a midsummer heatwave – is to engage in the serious study of Scotland's ancient Gaelic language. But plenty of the people listening so intently all around me to Bruce Gandy's music have taken a week or two out of their annual vacation and come here to Coeur d'Alene to do just that. And maybe, on reflection, their choice of venue is not quite so surprising as it might initially appear.

Gaelic may not be much associated nowadays with the American West. But it was, in fact, the common speech of some of the first Europeans to settle hereabouts in the early nineteenth century. Those pioneers were among the many Scottish Highlanders in the pay of the Montreal-based North West Company and its various competitors; men who had been born in Wester Ross, Argyll, the Hebrides; men who, in the years around 1800, steered their birch bark canoes down the great rivers which traverse the vast and scenically spectacular tract of territory lying between the Rockies and the shores of the Pacific.

One such was Angus MacDonald, a Canadian fur trader who belonged originally to Torridon and who came westward in the 1830s. Somewhere in the general vicinity of Coeur d'Alene he married a woman of the Nez Percé and was sufficiently accepted by her people to have become one of the few whites ever to participate in what MacDonald called the *san-ka-ha* – the 'red man's farewell,' as the far-travelled Gael explained, 'before he leaves for battle.'

To hear its 'thrilling notes ... sung by five or six hundred voices in a calm, starry night on the plains of Montana is a rare thing,' MacDonald wrote of this Nez Percé war chant. 'In 1850, at a great gathering of Indians to dance to this staid, insisting strain, I stripped with the leading men, painted with vermilion the grooves and dimples of my upper body, mounted my black buffalo charger with my full eagle feather cap and cantered round and round with them, keeping time to the song. This new sight of a white man to them and to myself they never forgot to speak of.'

Half a century later, when the fur trade was no more, when the Nez Percé

JIM MACLEOD FROM IDAHO

and all the several other neighbouring tribes had finally been broken by the US cavalry, when these native peoples had been confined to the reservations where many of them still live and when the newly formed states of Montana, Idaho and Washington were beginning to be developed by mining, logging and cattle-ranching interests, many more men and women of Highland extraction found employment in those parts.

Beside me, at a crowded table choc-a-bloc with Fort Ground Tavern beer glasses, sits the grandson of one of these early twentieth-century arrivals. His name is Jim MacLeod. He teaches English literature at North Idaho College, and he is the driving force behind the Scottish Studies Program which has brought me and so many others here to Coeur d'Alene.

'My father grew up in this part of the States,' Jim MacLeod informs me next morning. 'But he had been orphaned when he was just a kid. So all my dad could tell me about his own father, my grandfather, was that the old man had come out west to Montana in the early 1900s from Prince Edward Island.

Sometime before that, my dad thought, our people had emigrated to that part of Canada from the Isle of Skye in Scotland.'

We are talking in Jim MacLeod's office. Once it was part of the quarters occupied by the men in charge of the army detachments stationed at the immediately adjacent Fort Sherman – from which, incidentally, the Fort Ground Tavern derives its name – in the course of the many Indian Wars of the 1860s and 1870s. Now this well-weathered clapboard building, one of the oldest man-made structures in the Idaho panhandle, houses the mementoes gathered in the course of Jim MacLeod's quest for his family origins.

That quest, Jim recalls, began some twenty years ago with a trip to Prince Edward Island. This is one of the many areas in what are now Canada's Maritime Provinces to have been settled very largely by Highlanders; frequently by people expelled from Scotland on the instruction of those nineteenth-century landowners whose dubious distinction it was to have deliberately depopulated their estates in order to convert these enormously extensive properties into sheep farms.

Several generations on from the initial settlement, Gaelic lingers still in PEI and nearby Nova Scotia. So, too, does the age-old Highland interest in genealogy.

Thus it came about that, though he was equipped initially with only the most rudimentary knowledge of his PEI connections, Jim MacLeod was quickly put in touch with relatives of whose existence he had been previously quite unaware.

'From what I learned from my PEI kin,' Jim goes on, 'I was able to trace my family right back to Scotland.'

His grandfather had been wrong about the Isle of Skye, Jim now discovered; but not wildly wrong. The Montana pioneer's own grandfather, Jim's great-great-grandfather, came not from Skye but from the neighbouring, and much smaller, island of Raasay which this emigrant MacLeod had left in 1830.

Further investigation followed. Today, as a result, Jim MacLeod can boast a family tree which is firmly rooted in the eighteenth-century Hebrides, and which links this American college teacher with individuals as diverse as one of contemporary Canada's provincial premiers and modern Scotland's leading Gaelic poet, Sorley MacLean – the latter being one of the many people, on both sides of the Atlantic Ocean, who have helped sustain and fuel Jim MacLeod's continuing passion for all things relating to the Scottish Highlands.

As Coeur d'Alene's streets and sidewalks start to shimmer under yet another completely cloudless North American summer sky, Jim talks a little more about the intense emotional pull which is so obviously exerted on him by the altogether wetter, colder, windier – and, superficially at least, much less attractive – spot his ancestors were obliged to leave behind them nearly two whole centuries ago. 'I just love that place,' he says.

Later the same day, while seeking shelter from the sun under the tall trees now occupying the riverbank location where the US military's Fort Sherman previously stood, I think of what Jim has been saying; and I think, too, of all the many and varied individuals I have met who share something of Jim MacLeod's evidently fervent feelings for the Scottish Highlands.

There are the several friends I have made at this week's summer school in Coeur d'Alene. There are the other Highland enthusiasts I have got to know on earlier trips to both the United States and Canada. There are the ancestor-seeking Australians and New Zealanders I have encountered at different times in widely separated parts of Scotland itself. There are the numerous men and women who live still in localities like Islay, Sutherland or Lewis and who, in the face of the powerful social and economic pressures now endangering so many minority cultures right across the modern world, are making it their business to ensure that some part of their distinctive heritage will survive for at least another generation.

Why do the Scottish Highlands matter quite so much to such a surprisingly large, if now very widely scattered, segment of humanity?

This is too big a question, I conclude, for a hot and hazy July afternoon in the Idaho hill country. But it might be no bad thing for this particular Scottish Highlander, I reckon, to take a bit of time and, following the example set by Jim MacLeod, go off in search of information as to what it was that made us what we are.

Ulster in winter is a good deal less attractive than Idaho in summer. A chill and gusty wind is scraping and scratching at the sea which stretches eastward to my right. And although the morning is well advanced, daylight seems practically to have given up its struggle with the low clouds spilling thickly over the hilltops on my left.

In the little coastal towns of Ballygalley, Glenarm, Carnlough and Cushendall the main streets are scarcely any less deserted than the railinged promenades. Shopfront signs, draped in red tinsel, urge one and all to have a Merry Christmas. The few folk who are about, their collars turned up against the cold, do not look as if they are paying much attention.

Heading a mile or two inland, I stop my car at a spot which offers a wide view of hedged-in fields and isolated farmhouses. This is a comparatively modern countryside – the creation of the last three or four centuries. But above the limits of cultivation and enclosure are steep slopes and rocky precipices of a kind which have never been much altered by human activity. Focusing on these bare essentials of the Antrim landscape, I try to envisage how my surroundings would have appeared some fifteen hundred years ago.

In this part of Ireland, at about the time that Roman rule was drawing to a close in much of Europe, there lived a people who, if he could have encountered them, the nineteenth-century Montana fur trader, Angus MacDonald, would have found peculiarly familiar. Their language was one he would have recognised as a version of the common speech of his own West Highland boyhood. And in their customs, attitudes and outlook he would immediately have discerned much that reminded him of his life among the Nez Percé.

Those Antrim folk were Celts; outlying representatives of a tribal civilisation which, in the centuries immediately preceding Rome's imperial expansion, had made its mark on territories stretching from the British Isles to the Black Sea.

The Galatians to whom the Apostle Paul addressed one of his epistles were a Celtic people; so were the Gauls whom Julius Caesar conquered; so were those Adriatic warriors whose fearlessness is said to have so impressed the classical world's most justly renowned soldier, Alexander the Great.

The Celts, observed a coterie of Greek and Roman writers, were singularly dashing and flamboyant, brave and boastful, given to drink and relishing fine clothes and bodily decoration, fair-haired, red-haired, unbearably triumphant in their victories, rendered hopelessly downcast by a defeat. Their gods they worshipped, it was said, in oakwoods. Second only to their druidic priests, it was reported, Celtic tribes most honoured those bards or poets whose role it was to praise and dignify their chiefs.

Societies of this sort had long gone from most of mainland Europe by the fourth, fifth and sixth centuries of the Christian era; submerged first in the Roman Empire, swamped later by those Germanic invaders who so effectively seized the opportunity presented by Rome's precipitate decline. But Ireland had remained outside the Roman ambit, and external conquest, for the moment, did not threaten. Here in Antrim, then, a purely Celtic way of life continued; altered somewhat, to be sure, by its having recently made room for Christianity; but by no means so much changed as to have forgotten all the very many tales and sagas dealing with the Irish people's pagan antecedents.

This, the time of year when nights are longest, was the season of story-telling. This was when men heard again, around the winter's fire, of the heroic exploits of Cu Chulainn and how he singlehandedly protected Ulster from the war launched on the province by the men of Connaught. This, too, was when there was told once more the haunting tragedy of Deirdre – that most evocative, perhaps, of all the Ulster myths.

Deirdre's birth is preceded by dire prophecies of the havoc she will one day cause. But these auguries are defied by the aged king, Conchobar mac Nessa, who, desiring to keep the maiden's almost supernatural beauty to himself, has her raised in strict seclusion. But for all the king's efforts, of course, Deirdre falls in love with a young and handsome nobleman and flees with him to the sanctuary of another country lying not so far away across the sea. There word eventually comes to Deirdre and her lover that they can return quite safely now to Ireland. But this word, inevitably, proves false. Deirdre's man and his companions are treacherously slaughtered. And the distraught woman, rather than surrender herself finally to Conchobar, takes her life by dashing her own head against a rock.

From the exact spot on the Antrim coast near Ballycastle where the ill-fated Deirdre is reputed to have landed on her return to Ulster, I look out across the ocean to the land where she sought refuge.

In the language spoken by the first narrators of the Deirdre legend, the country over there was known as *Alba*. In that language, Gaelic, it is still Alba today. But the people who so named it, though they spoke of themselves as *Gaidheil*, or Gaels, were called *Scoti* by the Romans – who could be every bit as dismissive of local nomenclature as those French-Canadian explorers who so casually saddled North American tribes with wholly artificial labels such as Nez Percé. It is as Scoti, therefore, that the Gaels appear in the various Latin chronicles which provide us with some details of their early history. And it is as *Scotia*, or Scotland, that we know the nation which this people were one day to establish in the land where Deirdre was reputed to have fled.

All this is possibly complex enough. But it is indicative of the even more intricate nature of subsequent developments that this part of Ireland was eventually to be seized, nearly four hundred years ago now, by folk who, for all that they took no small pride in their claim to be Scots, had not only given up their own variant of Gaelic but were also so little enamoured of Gaels as to regard the still Gaelic-speaking Irish (whose lands they brutally expropriated) with that mixture of contempt and fear which this settler population's descendants still tend to display in their dealings with those other Ulster men and women whose forebears are to be found among the victims of this seventeenth-century colonisation.

Just how these convoluted realignments came about is one of this book's themes; for their beginnings are to be found in the extent to which the culture and language of the original *Scoti* – for all the latter's success in imposing their rule, for a period of several centuries, on practically all of Alba – were finally to become associated very largely with the part of Scotland we call the Highlands and Islands. Scottish Highlanders remained Gaels. Scottish Lowlanders did not.

So it transpired that, for all that they had earlier created both the Scottish state and the Scottish monarchy, Scotland's Gaels, or Highlanders, as they now came to be called, found themselves increasingly disregarded by their Lowland compatriots. And not only disregarded. When, in the period of religious strife which followed on the sixteenth-century Reformation, it was decided, in both London and Edinburgh, to replace the Irish Catholics of Ulster, in part at least, with Protestants imported from the Scottish Lowlands, this was merely to adapt to a new purpose a strategy first devised in an attempt to extirpate the Gaelic-speaking population of the Hebrides – that population being reckoned, by the Scottish and English governments of the day, to be every bit as unreliable, untrustworthy and dangerous as those other Gaelic-speaking communities which the Ulster colonisation policy was intended to eliminate.

This may be why, as a Scottish Highlander engaged in searching out my people's origins, I find it difficult to feel at home in modern Antrim. The endlessly aggressive Britishness of the district – with its deliberately flaunted Union Jacks and its red-white-and-blue painted village pavements – somehow seems to me offensive. For all that I am a Scot, and a Protestant Scot at that, I much prefer the more explicitly Gaelic Ireland that you find across the United Kingdom's borders with the Irish Republic. After all, it was with Ireland's Gaels, and not with the comparative newcomers who now constitute the loyalist and unionist majority in Britain's one remaining Irish enclave, that Scottish Highlanders traditionally identified. We had come, we knew, from Gaelic Ireland. And to Gaelic Ireland, over very many centuries, we regularly and habitually returned.

The fifth-century disintegration of the Roman Empire set whole European populations on the move. Most of the consequent migrations were of people heading east to west in the manner of the Goths, the Vandals and the Franks on the continental mainland; in the manner, too, of those Angle and Saxon tribes who, leaving their previous homelands in what is now north-western Germany, began to annex much of Britain's North Sea coast between the

GLEN ETIVE, ARGYLL, AN AREA ASSOCIATED WITH THE LEGEND OF DEIRDRIE

English Channel and the Firth of Forth. But there was eastward movement also. And its starting point was Ireland.

Irish emigrants established outposts at this time in modern Pembrokeshire, in modern Galloway and in modern Argyll. Of these three colonies, however, it was the last – eventually called Dalriada – which proved by far the most important; for it was to be the means of opening up other, and much more extensive, territories to Irish influence.

This longer-term significance of the Dalriadan settlement was not immediately apparent. Indeed, the future of the northern half of Britain seemed very much more likely, in the period of Rome's collapse, to lie with peoples other than those Gaels, or Scots, who now began to make the short sea passage from the Antrim coast to the south-western corner of the Highlands and Islands.

Dalriada – its name deriving, incidentally, from the Antrim locality to which many of its earlier colonists belonged – was, for long enough, surrounded by more powerful neighbours. All prospect of expansion beyond the Clyde estuary was rendered impossible by successive kingdoms ruled by men whose language is best described as Welsh. Northwards and eastwards, meanwhile, were the still more spacious realms of the Picts, a people whose regional dominance had been in evidence since Roman times; a people, moreover, who were to prove more than a match for those recently arrived Germanic incomers, the Angles, who, as a result, were quite unable to expand their influence much beyond the Lothians.

For several centuries, then, the Gaels of Dalriada remained effectively confined within comparatively restricted boundaries – politically and militarily at risk, from time to time, of being wholly overwhelmed by the various larger nations round about. Kintyre was theirs; so, too, were Knapdale, Cowal, Lorne, Islay, Jura, Colonsay, Mull, Coll, Tiree, Morvern and Ardnamurchan. But that was all. Dalriada, from one end to the other, north to south or east to west, measured no more than a hundred of our modern miles.

This was big enough, however, to allow the Scots to replicate in their new country all the essential features of the social order with which they had been long familiar in Ulster: its customs; its beliefs; its organising principles; and not least, of course, its Gaelic language.

Much of this substantial Irish inheritance was to endure in Scotland for a thousand years or more. Some of it endures, indeed, into the present, in the sense, for example, that Gaelic continues to be spoken by Scots. In the sense, too, that it is still possible on the Scottish side of the North Channel and especially in the Hebrides, to come across surviving remnants of those endlessly retold legends concerned with the doings of the likes of Deirdre and her doomed compatriots.

The different Celtic nations have always made a virtue of thus conserving their own traditions. And prior to the various upheavals which have so altered and disrupted life in Gaelic Scotland in the course of the last two hundred years, needless to say, the many links between the Scottish present and the Irish past were even more carefully fostered and sustained than was subsequently to be the case. That is why there is nothing accidental or fortuitous about those resemblances which can be detected between the sixteenth and seventeenth-century Scottish Highlands, on the one hand, and sixth and seventh-century Dalriada, on the other.

The clan chieftains of the later era constantly insisted on their descent from the Ulster warrior aristocracy of more than a millennium before. And for all that the genealogies which were held to sustain these claims might not have been such as to withstand scientific scrutiny, the extent to which the typical Highland chief's prestige depended – even in the era of Shakespeare, Milton and the beginnings of American colonisation – on his ability to claim kinship with the more notable kings and princes of ancient Ireland is itself indicative of the grip which their culture's Irish origins exerted on the Scottish Highland imagination.

Still more dependent than their chieftainly patrons on the maintenance of a society which, as their verse constantly stressed, derived much of its value system from Cu Chulainn's Ulster were the Gaelic bards who, in the Highlands and Islands of the 1600s and 1700s, fulfilled functions not at all dissimilar to those performed by their remote predecessors in Julius Caesar's Gaul.

Those bards – both as members of a highly status-conscious literary caste and as custodians of a continuity with which their own position was inextricably bound up – were naturally affected even more profoundly than the rest of Scotland's Gaels by the eventual shattering of the old order and the ensuing dispersal of so many of the people who had made that order what it was. Hence the elegiac, even apocalyptic, tone of some of the poetry which emanated from the Scottish Highlands in the period which saw Scottish Highlanders scattered hither and thither all around the globe.

Much of what had previously seemed indestructible, as the bards of that sad time suggested, was now utterly destroyed. But something, I think, of what had gone before remained; that something which impels a twentieth-century American like Jim MacLeod, for instance, to define his own identity – partially at least – in terms of his family's associations with those social and cultural traditions which had their genesis in Ulster.

Of all the many Gaels who made the voyage from Ireland to Dalriada, we have worthwhile biographical details of only one. From Antrim my route to his Donegal birthplace lies more or less due westward, through a gently undulating countryside cloaked in a frosty mist and smelling intermittently of the cattle slurry which farmer after farmer is spraying on his fields.

Donegal, too, was once regarded as a part of Ulster. But Ireland's partition in the 1920s resulted in the county joining the newly created Irish Republic and being separated, therefore, from the corner of the island which remained – as it still remains – under British jurisdiction. Now the fairly arbitrarily drawn line of national demarcation is one of the most contentious, and most bloodily disputed, frontiers in the world.

A few miles beyond Derry, my car bumps slowly through the border road-blocks. Soldiers stand in ones and twos behind sandbagged barricades, their automatic weapons permanently at the ready. Then, just past an empty customs post, brightly coloured roadside hoardings suddenly proliferate in a manner which is reminiscent of the United States. The road signs, however, are all in

Gaelic. Independent Ireland always seems to me to be both unfamiliar and very warmly welcoming.

The lights are coming on in Letterkenny and by the time I reach Lough Gartan, where a passing farmer tells me that the deserted heritage centre 'won't be opening much this side of Easter', an early dusk is making it difficult to tell one landscape feature from another.

Somewhere near here, tradition has it, there was born at just this time of year – on Thursday, 7 December AD 521, to be precise – a baby boy who was to be given the name Colum.

There is not now very much indication of this part of Donegal – a district of criss-crossing, narrow lanes and small, depopulated hamlets – ever having been a place inhabited by people of importance. But the little Colum's household, for all that it might have lacked the material grandeur which generally accompanies high social standing, was one of no small eminence all the same. The boy's mother was descended, it appears, from a certain *Cathair Mor*, King of Leinster. Still more significant, in the context of the times, was the fact that Colum's father was a great-grandson of none other than *Niall Noigiallach*, Niall of the Nine Hostages, whose clan or kindred, the *Ui Neill*, were the dominant political grouping in the north of Ireland of that day.

In his own lineage-obsessed community, then, the infant Colum would have been expected to become a man of consequence. What would have been more surprising, perhaps, was the way in which the growing boy, according to several of the many stories later told about him by his fellow Gaels, soon demonstrated an immense affinity for things ecclesiastical; to the point at which, it is said, his own contemporaries began to call him *Colum Cille*, meaning Colum of the Church.

It is as Colum Cille that the man I have thus tracked down to this cold, windy loughside, here in Donegal, is known to Gaelic-speakers still. Others are usually more familiar with the Latin version of his name, Columba. This translates as dove, something which might seem happily appropriate in that the bearer of the designation in question was eventually to become one of the Celtic world's most acclaimed and revered saints. In truth, however, there was precious little that was dovelike, quiet or peaceable about the career of Colum Cille. He was kin to princes, soldiers, warriors, and it showed.

Entering one of those monastic communities which became the principal means by which Ireland gave its own characteristic twist to the Christian faith it had begun to acquire in the century preceding Colum Cille's birth, the young

THE CALLANISH STONES, ISLE OF LEWIS

Columba seemed set, at first, on a life of broadly conventional piety. When still in his early twenties, he established – at a spot in Derry occupied now by one of the numerous Irish and Scottish churches, of practically all denominations, which are still dedicated to him – his first monastery. Other such foundations quickly followed. But Colum Cille's many secular involvements expanded also. One way or another, so it seems, his twin roles of churchman and politician became so intermingled as to result in his possibly having gone to war on behalf of his Ui Neill relations.

West of Lough Gartan, the Donegal countryside is harder, rougher, less domesticated than further east. An overnight hoar-frost is slowly melting with the rising of a watery winter's sun. The hillsides have that pallid, rain-bleached look which the Scottish Highlands also take on this late in the year.

Gleann Colm Cille might be in the Hebrides. It has the long and narrow fields of our own crofting townships, the same strong scent of peatsmoke, the same clumps of wind-distorted trees, the same sheep; even, if you were to judge solely by the faces of the one or two folk to be seen this chilly morning, the same people.

An Atlantic swell is breaking heavily in a sandy bay. And here in Gleann Colm Cille, as in so many parts of my own country, there are everywhere the ruins which show this to have been previously a much more densely populated place. The Irish, like the Scottish Highlanders, all too often left a long time ago for North America.

On my car radio, as I make for Killybegs and Ballyshannon, I listen to a Gaelic news broadcast of the same type as I might pick up at home in Skye. From another local station, interspersed only with repeated injunctions to take advantage of the many Christmas bargains to be got in Donegal town, comes a steady stream of US country music – as popular in Ireland as in Scotland and, if you have an ear for such things, still shaped partly by its origins among the Scots and Irish settlers of Kentucky and the Appalachians.

Moving on south, I pause briefly at Drumcliff in County Sligo. A round tower by the roadside and a slender Celtic cross in the Church of Ireland graveyard which also contains the burial place of William Butler Yeats, whose poetry drew no small part of its inspiration from this locality, are all that remain now of one of Colum Cille's many monasteries.

Somewhere hereabouts, in 561, when Colum Cille was well into his middle age as those things were then reckoned, there took place the battle of Cul Drebene, a particularly bloody conflict, so the surviving evidence suggests, between the Ui Neill and those other kindreds who, at the time, were seeking to expand their own power and authority.

Colum Cille, himself an Ui Neill aristocrat as well as an increasingly important cleric, is claimed in some accounts to have actually taken part in the battle – something which would have been in breach of his ecclesiastical commitments. Certainly he was deeply implicated in the politicking which inevitably surrounded confrontations of the Cul Drebene type. There may, therefore, be some connection between the fighting here in Sligo and the persistent belief that Columba, by way of penance for sins of some considerable magnitude, was expelled from Ireland by his fellow churchmen.

Whether ordered out or not, Colum Cille now left Ulster, as Deirdre was considered to have done before, for Alba – setting sail from Derry, it is generally agreed, in 563 and taking with him, it is said, the twelve men whom he had chosen to accompany him on his Scottish mission. Theirs was a journey which is still remembered by the Gaels.

Once clear of Lough Foyle, which connects Derry with the open sea, the little party's course lay something east of north. Behind them, and becoming less distinct with every passing minute, was the fifty-mile stretch of coastline separating Malin Head in County Donegal from Fair Head in County Antrim. Ahead, and to their right, was Islay, its green and grassy western slopes – so much at odds with the steep and barren looking peaks of Jura to their rear – clearly indicating the fertility which was to make the island the most consistently prized, and most bitterly fought over, of all the Hebrides.

Columba's vessel was a *curach*, or coracle, made from roughly waterproofed ox hides stretched over a wooden frame. The *curach* was not, by later standards, a very sturdy craft, but it was light and manoeuvrable. It was to be used by Irish fishermen until the present century. And it was capable of voyages much longer than that being made by Colum Cille and his dozen comrades.

The Vikings, who were subsequently to follow the oceanic routes which monks of the Columban Church initially explored, gave the name of *papar*, priests, to the Gaelic-speaking clergy they encountered – and occasionally killed – in so many remote locations. Hence the manner in which the Norse-derived names of numerous islands, strung out across much of the North Atlantic, serve still as a memorial to men whose ceaseless spiritual questings took them, quite literally, to the edge of the known world. There is a Pabbay (priest-island) to the south of Barra, another to the east of Skye and a third between Harris and North Uist. Orkney has its Papa Stronsay and Papa Westray, Shetland its Papa Stour. The island of Papey, to the south-east of Iceland, is one more testimony to this monkish wanderlust, as is Pappabyli on the Icelandic mainland.

An equally far-travelled Irish churchman (but one whose journeyings happened to take him east and south rather than north and west) was subsequently to set down, for the benefit of the Frankish monarch in whose court he found himself, how he had talked with one of those monastic voyagers who, having first sailed through the Hebrides, had made the ocean crossing to Faroe which he had reached, the monk said, some two days after leaving the 'northernmost islands of Britain'. From Faroe to Iceland – where ninth-century colonisers from Norway were to discover the abandoned 'books, bells and croziers' of the monastic communities they displaced – would have entailed another two or three days at sea. And beyond Iceland, of course, lay Greenland and America.

The Vikings were certainly to establish themselves in Greenland and to make intermittent contact with the American localities they named Markland and Vinland. But there are those who still believe, on the basis both of its undoubted practicability and of various hints which can be discerned in the tales surrounding the exploits of the more notable monastic sailors of Columba's time, that the Gaels had preceded the Norsemen even here; that they, not the Vikings, were the first Europeans to catch sight of the New World; just as they assuredly constituted the earliest settlers of those other North Atlantic lands which the Norsemen were later to make permanently Scandinavian.

The sea, at all events, held no particular terrors for Colum Cille and his companions. To them, as to the Hebridean population ever since, it was a familiar element; one which looms large in Gaelic song and poetry and one over which the expedition putting out from Derry needed none of the miraculous storm-stilling powers, later attributed to Columba, to exercise a degree at least of mastery.

A very ancient verse, long believed to have been composed by Colum Cille himself, reflects on the speed of his coracle, its stern turned decisively on Derry, its prow pointing purposefully towards Alba. Columba, in the vessel's stern, gazes ever southward. And 'large is the tear' in the churchman's 'soft grey eye' as he looks back, for what he expects to be the last time, on the country of his birth.

Whatever it was that had driven Colum Cille from Ireland, then, the sense of exile is strong in the traditions dealing with his coming to Scotland. He had, or so the story goes, to guard against even catching sight again of Erin. So now he sailed past Islay and Jura, Oronsay and Colonsay, from all of which the Irish mountains can readily be glimpsed on the horizon, and made his landfall at last on Iona. From there no part of Ireland can be seen.

CHAPTER TWO

Columba is said to have set foot on Iona at a spot known still as Port na Curaich, coracle harbour. One of a set of diminutive coves on the island's south-western coast, Port na Curaich offers little shelter from winter gales, the worst of which usually emanate from that direction. But its very exposure has resulted in a steeply shelving shingle beach little short of ideal, on a day of gentler winds, for effecting a landing in those more fragile sorts of craft which, being vulnerable to wave damage, are best dragged beyond the line of the high tide. The coracle containing Colum Cille and his companions would have been virtually ashore here before it touched bottom, and to get it clear of the sea would have been the work of moments only.

For more than two hundred years now – ever since that astonishingly robust old reactionary, Samuel Johnson, made his way to the Hebrides in the hope of discovering in the islands a surviving example of those patriarchal social orders which, to Johnson's evident chagrin, had elsewhere been extinguished by the rampant commercialism and industrialism which were so transforming eighteenth-century Britain – tourists and travel writers have expounded, as Samuel Johnson did himself, on the peculiar qualities of Iona; its sense of sanctity; its peacefulness; the extent to which it seems a place apart.

I do not think Iona would have struck Colum Cille like that; not initially at least. A monk he most certainly was, and, at times, something of a mystic. But Columba did not come here solely to engage in introspection. He sought to change the world much more than he ever sought to meditate upon it. He wished, above all other things, to have authority, indeed power, to exert some influence still in Ireland, to shape the pattern of events in Dalriada and to gain a foothold in the Pictish realms beyond Dalriada's northern and eastern boundaries.

These were far-reaching ambitions; indicative, some would say, of motives not becoming in a churchman. But that is to impose on Colum Cille our own contemporary distinction between the secular and the ecclesiastical; a distinction which sixth-century people would have found quite incomprehensible. Politicking of the type in which he had engaged already in Ireland and in which he was to engage further in Scotland was, to Columba, a perfectly legitimate, even essential, means of securing the position of the still fragile faith to which he had dedicated himself. And so Colum Cille, on making his first inspection of Iona, was probably less concerned with its potential for promoting spiritual renewal than he was with its more down-to-earth attributes – above all, with the island's capacity to serve as the headquarters of a monastic community capable of making the widest possible impact on the world of his day.

As can be seen still by visiting the various Highlands and Islands localities where they chose to base themselves – places like Lismore or Applecross – the Celtic Church's monks had an unerring eye as to the agricultural quality of a piece of land. They always chose the best available. And Iona did not disappoint in this regard.

The welcoming patch of green and springy turf above the shore at Port na Curaich is a good beginning. After a couple of hundred yards, admittedly, it gives way to the hillocky, hummocky landscape which is characteristic of so much of this part of Scotland. Wiry heather and a little bracken grow on the drier knolls. The hollows are boggy and marshy. Your boots squelch beneath you here even in the driest weather. And while such areas offer some rough pasture, they provide almost nothing in the way of plots that can be cropped. Columba, on the day of his arrival in Iona, would not have lingered long in this part of the island.

The ground rises gradually as you walk north from Port na Curaich. Then, not far beyond the little loch which serves now as Iona's reservoir, it drops away steeply to reveal a great swathe of grassland which completely spans the island at its centre. This is machair. It is the single most distinctive contribution which the Hebrides make to the ecology of our planet, for there is nothing else quite like it anywhere on earth.

Here and there in Lewis, more generally in Harris, and more universally still in islands like the Uists, Barra, Vatersay, Tiree and Iona, the sea and wind together have carried far inland great quantities of glittering white sand which, when you run it through your fingers, can be seen to consist of the crushed and pulverised remnants of innumerable shells. This sand is rich in calcium carbonate. It neutralises and fertilises the highly acidic peat with which it comes in contact. All manner of herbs and flowers flourish everywhere on the resulting soils. The overall effect, rendered still more striking by the unproductive nature of the surrounding landscape, is approximately equivalent to that more normally associated with an oasis in the desert.

The day I made my way from Port na Curaich, the first place which I visited in the course of writing this book, was a Thursday. This, to the Gaels of Scotland, has long been *Diardaoin Chaluim-Chille*, Columba's day, the point in the week at which it was thought lucky to begin an undertaking. And though my being on Iona that particular Thursday, was – to be honest – quite fortuitous, I could not have chosen a better time to make the trip.

It was June. And it was one of those days which are not uncommon in the islands at that time of year; a day of ceaseless sun; a day of light breezes from the north; a day of vivid colours. If it was on such a day that Columba walked from Port na Curaich, by way of Loch Staonaig, then his feelings, on reaching the flanks of Cnoc Druidean and looking out across Iona's western machair, must have been those of a man who was beginning to be convinced that, in selecting this island, he had made an excellent choice.

The bay below the machair is Camas Cuil an t-Snaimh. Its waters, because of the light reflected back from the shellsand on the seabed, have a turquoise tint. The dunes are white as snow. The machair is awash with buttercups and daisies. There is a constant noise of birdsong.

Iona's crofts, of which I can see four from the rock on which I have seated myself, were laid out in the early nineteenth century. But the land here has been worked constantly since the time of Colum Cille, and it clearly gives a good return. There are big and healthy cattle to be seen in one part of the machair. Elsewhere sheep are grazing. The island lambs look to be doing well.

The eighteenth-century agriculturalist John Walker, who visited Iona at much the same time as Samuel Johnson, but whose report on the place was of an altogether more prosaic kind, pronounced Iona's plains, as he called the machair, 'very fertile'. And for all the island's northerly location, Walker observed, 'the heat of the summer, with the warm nature of the soil, proves sufficient to produce more early crops than in most parts of Britain'.

Walker was right. The year's longest day has not yet been reached, but already one of Iona's crofters has cut and harvested a hefty crop of silage.

I head out across the machair, more than a mile wide at this point, and begin to climb the hills beyond. My destination is Dun I, the island's highest point. At under 350 feet it is not very much of a mountain, but it is the obvious spot from which to view both Iona and its surroundings. It seems likely, therefore, that Columba, too, turned his footsteps towards Dun I in the course of his original reconnaissance of the island.

From Dun I's summit Colum Cille would have confirmed his first impressions of Iona. Towards the island's northern tip is another extensive tract of machair. On the east, above the sound which separates Iona from the adjacent, and much larger, island of Mull, are more green fields. This place, Columba must have concluded, was capable of feeding the community he now made up his mind to establish here. And on looking at the wider scene, on first taking in that enormously extended crescent of islands and mountains which can be seen so readily from Dun I on a day of even reasonable visibility, Colum Cille must have felt still surer that his choosing of Iona was correct. Here he could feel himself to be at the centre of things.

It is on this point, of course, that our modern perceptions of the island are

MAN AND DOG, ISLE OF SKYE

likely to be most at odds with those of the man commemorated still in its common Gaelic name, *I Chaluim-Chille*. Today the Hebrides are usually thought to be anything but central. They might be more accurately described as peripheral, for the way we organise our world has made them so.

Had I come to Iona directly from Derry, as Columba did, I should have had to begin by driving east, by way of Coleraine and Ballymena, to Larne, not far from Belfast. There I should have taken the ferry to Stranraer in Galloway. Then my route would have lain northwards, on indifferent roads, to Girvan, Ayr and Glasgow. Beyond Glasgow, there would have been another lengthy drive along the shores of Loch Lomond and through the various glens and passes on the westward route to Oban. At Oban I would have boarded the ferry for Mull. On landing at Craignure I would have turned south for Fionnphort. There I should have parked my car, taken the passenger-only boat to Iona and set out on the hour-long walk to Port na Curaich.

The entire journey would have involved three separate sea crossings and the traversing of several hundred miles of road. It could not be accomplished in less than two days and, at certain times of year, might well take three.

In Colm Cille's time, however, to travel from Derry to Iona involved a single trip of no more than one hundred miles; the sort of trip which the crew of a coracle, given anything like a fair wind, could easily accomplish between the rising and the setting of a single summer sun.

Iona, at a time when the sea could be much more conveniently and rapidly crossed than the adjacent land – which was to remain almost wholly roadless for another thousand years – was much more accessible some fourteen or fifteen centuries ago than is the case today. And not only could the island be reached more readily in the distant past; it was, psychologically as well as geographically, much less isolated then than now. For, while Iona's physical position has not altered in the intervening period, political and cultural relationships between the Highlands and Islands, on the one hand, and the rest of Britain, on the other, have changed massively. They have done so to the disadvantage of places like Columba's island.

The modern writers who dwell so habitually on Iona's unapproachability have come here, by necessarily complicated means of the type I have already described, from those cities which we now regard, inevitably, as being the key components of our society. They have travelled to the island from Edinburgh, from Birmingham, from London. And it generally seems to them that, in making their long journeys to the Hebrides, they have left civilisation behind. That is reasonable enough. Though we might, from time to time, wish to make our escape to the likes of Iona, and though we might – in this particular context – value such localities precisely because they differ so much from what we regard as standard, we would not want, by and large, to live permanently in the way that island people live. Such people, it is commonly said, are actually deprived; the degree of their deprivation being measured by the extent to which their communities are denied those things which, in towns, are taken mostly for granted; speedy communications; good schools; swimming pools; shops; public libraries. There are few such facilities in the more rural parts of the Highlands and Islands. So the region, on any scale of what it is that constitutes an acceptable mode of life in the Britain of the 1990s, tends to be placed always near the bottom.

The Hebrides today, then, are truly on the margins. They are far from our centres of national authority; they are difficult to reach; they are lacking in the various amenities which, in the minds of most of us, make it possible to have a reasonable existence. Their populations do not generally possess the electoral clout required to ensure that public policy, which is invariably formulated elsewhere, takes account of their particular needs and aspirations.

So it has been for many generations. And so long and so completely have the people of the Highlands and Islands been at the mercy of essentially external agencies – ranging from the exploitative landlords of the nineteenth century to the frequently uncaring governments of the twentieth – that it seems hardly believable now that the Hebrides were once the source of forces capable of setting history on a different course. But such was, in fact, the case. At the time of Colum Cille, and for several centuries afterwards, great events had their origins here.

Facing south-west or west, in the vicinity of the Dun I summit cairn, you are aware only of the open ocean. Turning to the north-west you look out on the low-lying islands of Tiree and Coll. Due north, and a good deal further off, are the peaks of Rum. Beyond them, barely visible and some sixty miles distant, are the mountains of Skye. To the north-east are the much closer hills of Mull – with the Ross of Mull, the name given to that island's southernmost penin-sula, no more than a mile away across the waters of the sound. South-east are Colonsay, Jura and Islay. And to the south, though there is no land to be seen, the eye can easily discern, in certain meteorological conditions, the shapes of clouds which the winds have caused to form over Ireland.

It is easy enough to imagine Columba gazing on these various panoramas. It is practically impossible to conceive of how different from ours was his understanding of the world which lay beyond that encircling horizon and to which the seaways from Iona were to give him such immediate access.

Nowadays, when even those of us whose homes are in the Highlands and Islands are inclined to take for granted that the more important intellectual and other influences shaping our lives almost always have their origins in the great cities of the south, it takes an immense effort to imagine how things would have seemed when that process of cultural diffusion operated in reverse; when the Gaels of Ireland and Dalriada – a people who were Christian and a people whose churchmen at least were able both to read and write – could aspire, as Colum Cille and his successors on Iona indubitably aspired, to bring the benefits of what they believed to be their superior civilisation to the frequently pagan and illiterate barbarians who, in the aftermath of imperial Rome's spectacular collapse, had invaded and conquered the territories to which a later age would give the name of England.

To Iona, Colm Cille is reported to have foretold, not only the kings of the Gaels, but kings of other nations also, would one day do 'great and special honour'. It was a prophecy which Columba himself did his utmost to bring to fruition; striving, with all the considerable strength of character at his disposal, to make his island community fit for the many vital tasks he had in mind for it.

There were buildings to be put up and timbers to be brought from the Scottish mainland. There was ploughing to be done and harvesting, cows to be milked, cloth to be woven, fish to be caught. There was mass to be celebrated and confession to be heard. There were important guests to be entertained and interviewed. There were holy books to be copied. There were expeditions to be mounted.

Contrary to legend, Columba did return occasionally to Ireland. But he gave more of his attention now to the Gaelic-speaking realm of which Iona itself was a part, dabbling constantly in the affairs of Dalriada and arranging, for example, to have one of its monarchs consecrated in his island abbey.

But Colum Cille was not content to have only Gaels within his sphere of influence. At Iona he received at least one deputation from the Welsh-speaking realm of Strathclyde. And from Iona he travelled, by way of the Firth of Lorne, Loch Linnhe and the Great Glen, to the court of the Pictish King Bridei somewhere in the vicinity of modern Inverness.

The heathen Picts – folk with their own language and their own customs – were not immediately converted by Columba. But the form of Christianity which they were eventually to adopt was the one which was preached by the monks and abbots of Iona.

This was equally true of the Northumbrians. Unlike the Picts, who had occupied many of the territories to the north of Hadrian's Wall in the era of the Roman Empire, the Northumbrians, in the manner of the Gaels themselves, were comparatively recent arrivals in Britain. Their origins lay on the far side of the North Sea. And the Northumbrians, like all such immigrants and colonisers from mainland Europe, were pagan. But their extensive territories, occupying much of what is now the north of England and the south of Scotland, were eventually to be Christianised by men of the Iona persuasion. And it was on Lindisfarne, yet another island, though this time a Northumbrian one, that there was constituted, in the early seventh century, a further monastic foundation of the Iona type – an establishment which, as a result of its successful fusion of Celtic and Continental influences, was to make its own highly distinctive contribution to the Columban inheritance.

Iona's growing authority among the Picts would one day make it easier for the royal house of Dalriada to incorporate that formerly independent people into the single, Gael-ruled state which would become known as Scotland. In Northumbria, however, events were to follow a very different course, one that was to ensure that all the various Saxon and Angle kingdoms in the more southern part of Britain would quickly cease to look to Iona for religious guidance.

In 597, the year in which Colum Cille died, there came to Kent, on the instructions of Gregory, Bishop of Rome, a missionary by the name of Augustine. This priest based himself in Canterbury, and it was principally from this new centre of spiritual endeavour, not from Iona, that Christianity first came to the southern part of England.

Soon Canterbury's influence had expanded into Northumbria also. The kingdom's rulers were consequently confronted with something of a dilemma. For the teachings of Canterbury, it was rapidly apparent, were by no means at one with those of Iona and Lindisfarne. Between the successors of Columba, on the one hand, and the successors of Augustine, on the other, there was total disagreement, for example, on issues such as the method to be employed to calculate the date of Easter. And since the feast of the Resurrection was the most critical event in the entire Christian calendar, this was no small matter.

To whom, then, was Northumbria to give its allegiance? To the Celtic Church whose observances it had followed since the men of Iona had first caused its earlier gods to be set aside in favour of Jesus and Jehovah? Or to the church of Canterbury which, being more directly linked with Rome, was increasingly thought to have access to greater ecclesiastical resources than were ever likely to be commanded by clerics whose roots lay in Dalriada and Ireland?

DONALD MACDONALD, TARBERT, LOCH NEVIS

ESTATE WORKER, GLEANN GEAL, MORVERN

LINDA MACGILLIVRAY, CROFTER, ISLE OF MULL

JOHN MACINNES, IONA

NORMAN GILLIES, SABHAL MOR OSTAIG, ISLE OF SKYE

INNES MACCOLL IN HIS SHOP AT DUROR

BALALLAN, LEWIS

JOAN MACINNES, DUIRINISH, LOCHALSH

JOHN FRANCIS MACEACHAN, SOUTH UIST

FISHERMAN MAKING FOR HOME, SOUTH UIST

SALMON FISHERMEN, SKEABOST, ISLE OF SKYE

MALLAIG

KENNETH MACKENZIE, SOUTH UIST

At a great synod, or conference, held in Whitby in 664 the rival claims of the two contending parties were debated. The decision went to Canterbury. And its writ now ran – as it has, one way or another, ever since – in every part of England.

In the following century a very eminent English churchman, one Bede by name, would record these events in the history he composed in his monastery at Jarrow. His own loyalty to Canterbury was beyond question. And he had no doubt as to the Iona community's having made mistakes in their determining of the great Christian festivals. They had 'none to bring them the synodal decrees for the observance of Easter', Bede explained charitably of the Iona men's failure to fall into line with Roman practice, 'by reason of their being so far away from the rest of the world'. Having thus excused him from any blame as to such errors as may have been made by his church, the Englishman then went out of his way to pay proper tribute to Colum Cille. 'This we know for certain,' Bede observed of Columba, 'that he left successors renowned for their continency, their love of God and their observance of the monastic rites.' It was an epitaph, I think, with which Colum Cille would not have been displeased; the more so since it was delivered in one of those faraway nations he had been so anxious to bring within Iona's ambit.

Of those who came after Columba at Iona the most outstanding was Adomnan, the seventh-century abbot whose biography of his more famous predecessor is our single most important source of information about the early history of the Scottish Highlands. Adomnan, of course, was a highly biased author. The principal aim of his book about the Iona community's founder was to portray Colum Cille as the holiest of holy men: a worker of miracles; a priest in direct communication with his God; a person eminently worthy of the sainthood which Adomnan, for one, was determined to bestow on him. Nobody should turn to Adomnan's *Life of Columba* in the expectation of finding there an objective chronicle of the age with which it deals.

But something of Colum Cille's nature and outlook nevertheless emerges from this thirteen-hundred-year-old account of the many and varied doings of the enduringly fascinating human being whom Adomnan habitually calls 'the blessed man'.

That Columba was both proud and imperious is not in doubt; that he desired to make his mark on history is obvious; that he succeeded in so doing is more than evident. But his ambitions, while they were – in one way – worldly enough, did not take a typical earthly form. He had no use for riches or the common trappings of great wealth. He sought no high office. He lived all his life in turf and stone cells of the kind which were inhabited by the lowliest of monks. He took his turn at manual labour. And he toiled all his days in the scriptorium, or writing house, where monastic penmen, of whom Iona possessed some of the most skilled in the world, ensured the transmission of all sorts of learning – by no means all of it theological – from one generation to the next.

The brilliantly illuminated manuscripts which were thus produced constitute one of the more outstanding achievements of Gaelic civilisation. And in the way in which their creators employed traditional – and thus pagan – motifs to decorate and beautify the parchment pages on which they so painstakingly copied and recopied the gospels, there can be glimpsed something of the extent to which the Celtic Church embodied and carried forward much that derived from sources other than Christianity.

A similar intermingling of influences is to be seen in the slender stone crosses which were to become one of the still recognisable trade marks of the Gaelic-speaking religious orders. And this notably easygoing approach to what had been inherited from the past – an approach which was so much more self-confident and outward-looking than that adopted by those fearful and narrow-minded Presbyterian evangelicals who, in the nineteenth century, were to decree that to take even the most casual interest in Gaeldom's stories, songs and legends was to prove one's utter worthlessness – is reflected, too, in the fact that it is to monasteries of the sort which Colum Cille established that we owe the survival, in written form, of those sagas in which the people of Ireland and Dalriada embodied the ancient myths of their race.

Thus it came about that Europe's oldest vernacular literature consists of the lengthy Gaelic tales which celebrate the deeds of Cu Chulainn, Oisin, Diarmait, Maeve and Deirdre. Some of those slowly unfolding dramas deal in very bloody stuff. Many, however, are more concerned with love and steadfastness than they are with the waging of war. And in the form in which they were set down by the scribes of the Columban church, it is notable that – in contrast, once again, to so much of what has been presented as received religion in the Highlands and Islands of more modern times – they take a singularly benign view of humanity's purpose on this earth. No hellfire of the sort on which so many Hebridean preachers have dwelt so droolingly in the course of the last two hundred years was ever envisaged by the compilers of those first Gaelic epics. Their moral universe was one in which the after-life is characterised much less by suffering than by eternal youth and promise.

There would come a time when Christian missionaries, labouring in places like Africa, would insist on potential converts severing all links with their own tribal traditions. The first step to be taken by those wishing to achieve salvation, the Victorians were inclined to think, was to adopt the Western way of life. This was why getting bare breasts safely under whalebone corsets sometimes seemed rather more important, to the typical topee-clad churchman, than the propagation of the scriptures. But Christianity was brought to Scotland, as it had been brought to Ireland, by clerics who were much more closely integrated than their more recent successors with the peoples they were endeavouring to win for God. The monks of the Celtic Church were endlessly accommodating, preferring compromise to conflict and always trying to reconcile their novel creed with earlier convictions.

Men of Colum Cille's stamp did not denigrate folk culture. They recorded it, and, recognising that they would not otherwise make much progress in winning souls for Christ, they willingly made room in their own system of beliefs for innumerable features of much older faiths.

The well-known physical attributes of Celtic goddesses became subtly intermingled with those of the Virgin Mary. The natural springs which had long been worshipped by both Gael and Pict were associated with the saints of the Columban Church. There was a convenient blurring of the distinction between what was properly miraculous and what was merely magical, between faith and superstition.

So matters were to continue in the Highlands and Islands for another thousand years. 'They all of them have a remarkable propensity to whatever is marvellous and supernatural,' it was noted by John Walker of Iona's population – who were, by then, ostensibly Protestant – in the 1770s. 'They are famous for the second sight; full of visions seen either by themselves or others; and have many wild and romantick notions concerning religion and invisible things.'

In Walker's time, as for several decades afterwards, Iona men and women would gather on the Thursday before Easter in order to watch one of their number wade waist-deep into the Atlantic and there pour a basin of porridge into the salt water. To make such a gift to the ocean, it was believed, would ensure a plentiful supply of the cast-up seaweed needed for the manuring of the island's fields. This ceremony, local tradition has it, took place in the vicinity of the little hill known as Dun Mhannannain. That hill shares its name with one of the Celtic gods of the sea.

Nor were such survivals limited to Iona. Into the nineteenth century, and even into the twentieth, there were to be found in the Highlands and Islands people who spoke still of Deirdre's beauty as a thing of wonder; people who were reluctant to give up the observance of customs that were old when Columba was born in Donegal.

The Free Church and the Church of Scotland – maybe more rationalist, and certainly less tolerant, in this respect at least, than the Iona monks – invariably condemned such attitudes. But these persisted very stubbornly, not least among the Presbyterian clergy's own adherents. So it was that when – as a boy growing up on the shores of a loch that had been known to Colum Cille – I was taken out to fish by my father and my grandfather, one of my first lessons in rowing concerned the absolute necessity of always turning our boat in a clockwise direction. To do otherwise, it was explained to me, would be to offend against the pattern established by the sun. In this way I was taught something that others of my age had learned in the Celtic world long before the life and death of Jesus.

In an ancient Irish manuscript now stored in the Burgundian Library in Brussels there is to be found a Gaelic poem which the document's compiler explicitly attributed to St Columba. The existence of such a poem would have come as no surprise to those Highlands and Islands story-tellers who traditionally insisted, over the centuries, that Colum Cille was a bard of note in his own language. And while there is no way now of confirming Columba's actual authorship of the verses in question, they are obviously the work of someone with a great affection for the Hebrides; someone who recalls the times he has spent so happily on the seashore, walking by the water's edge and listening to the sounds of gulls and sandpipers; someone who remembers the pleasures of fishing; someone who wishes to hear again 'the thunder of the crowding waves upon the rocks' and 'the roar by the side of the church of the surrounding sea'.

There is, in that poem, the sheer delight in things natural that one finds in some of the oldest Gaelic tales and some of the most recent Gaelic writing. Though there is no proof that its lines are those of Colum Cille, neither is there any proof that they are not. A man who was accustomed to sit for hours together on the hill above his Iona monastery, gazing out on his surroundings; a man who clearly came to love this island; a man whose skill with words was beyond question: such a man could well have set down such a tribute to his place.

On a summer Saturday in 597, writes Adomnan, the now elderly Columba went with his attendant, Diarmait, to a barn belonging to their monastery. There he blessed two heaps of newly winnowed corn and confided to his servant that this was to be his last day in the world. Walking back to his cell, Colum Cille, 'bowed down with old age', was forced to sit and 'rest a little'. As he sat, continues Adomnan, 'there came up to him a white pack-horse, the same that was used, as a willing servant, to carry the milk-vessels from the cowshed to the monastery, and, strange to say, laid its head on his bosom and began to utter plaintive cries.'

The daylight hours went by. Columba, climbing to his favourite vantage point for the last time, placed one more benediction on Iona. He resumed his copying of the psalm which he had for some days been transcribing. He made his way to the abbey church for evening service. And he returned to the bare stone slab that was his bed.

'Then as soon as the bell tolled at midnight,' says Adomnan, 'he rose hastily and went to the church. Running more quickly than the rest, he entered it alone and knelt down in prayer before the altar. At the same time his attendant, Diarmait, who more slowly followed him, saw from a distance that the whole interior of the church was filled with a heavenly light in the direction of the saint. But as he drew near to the door, the same light he had seen, and which was also seen by a few more of the brethren standing at a distance, quickly disappeared.

'Diarmait, entering the church, cried out in a mournful voice: "Where art thou, father?" And feeling his way in the darkness, as the brethren had not yet brought in the lights, he found the saint lying before the altar; and raising him up a little, he sat down beside him and laid his holy head on his bosom.

'Meanwhile, the rest of the monks ran in hastily in a body with their lights and, beholding their dying father, burst into lamentations. And the saint, as we have been told by some who were present, even before his soul departed, opened wide his eyes and looked round him from side to side, with a countenance full of wonderful joy and gladness, no doubt seeing the holy angels coming to meet him.

'Diarmait then raised the holy right hand of the saint that he might bless his assembled monks. And the venerable father himself moved his hand at the same time, as well as he was able; that, as he could not in words, while his soul was departing, he might at least, by the motion of his hand, be seen to bless the brethren. And having given them his holy benediction in this way, he immediately breathed his last.'

That night in Donegal, as the young Adomnan had heard directly from one of the miracle's witnesses, a group of men who were netting fish in a river not far from Colum Cille's birthplace, saw a great light in the heavens; a light which 'illuminated the whole earth like the summer sun at noon'. Columba, these men knew, was dead. That he had enjoyed God's special favour few folk doubted, then or later. His cult was consequently to endure for a long time.

King after king was buried in Iona. And there is no lack of tales as to how, in times of stress and trouble, Colum Cille came to men of power in dreams and visions, among them King Oswald of Northumbria in the seventh century and Alexander II, King of Scots, in the thirteenth.

Certain relics of Columba – some fragments of a bone, perhaps, a lock of hair or something of that kind – were kept carefully for centuries in a highly decorated casket, or reliquary, which, though empty now, can still be seen in Edinburgh. And when, on occasions of great national emergency, this most precious and sacred of objects was carried with the Scottish army – as it was, for example, to Bannockburn on the day in 1314 that Robert Bruce confronted the English forces sent to destroy both his and Scotland's claims to independence – then victory, it was thought, would be assured.

Many years afterwards, when Scotland had a king no longer and when the Gaels had become a harried set of peasant fishermen and farmers, subject daily to eviction from the lands their ancestors had begun to settle in Columba's time, there were still among them men and women who prayed habitually to Colum Cille for aid. Whether or not he sent to them the help they needed, they made an appropriate choice. If to be a Scottish Highlander is – as this book maintains – to have some connection with, or feeling for, the Gaelic-speaking people who first came here from Ireland, then Columba was one of the earliest of us and, perhaps, the greatest.

Coming down Dun I on its eastern side, I soon reach Iona Abbey. This is a twentieth-century recreation of a medieval original. It owes nothing to the altogether simpler structures raised by Colum Cille and he would, I think, have found it oppressively ornate. But that thought, maybe, owes rather less to what I know of Columba than it does to my own Highland Protestant upbringing. In Iona Abbey, just as in Notre Dame or in Westminster, I tend to feel a little bit uneasy. The Calvinist in me, it seems, is never going to be at home with lavish churchly decoration.

The Iona brotherhood created by Colum Cille was brought effectively to an end, in the early part of the ninth century, by the Vikings. But another has now taken its place – the ecumenical community established here in 1938 by George MacLeod. A pacifist and socialist to whom the reconstruction of Iona was a means of resolving something of his gnawing disenchantment with what appeared to him to be the growing spiritual sterility of the mainstream Church of Scotland, MacLeod – who was descended from a long line of Gaelic-speaking ministers – had one quality at least in common with Columba. When

HOUSE BY THE SHORE

Colum Cille raised his voice in anger with those Iona monks who failed to measure up to his exacting standards, his words, so it is said traditionally, could be heard by people working in their fields in Mull. George MacLeod, who was every bit as convinced as Columba that he was in charge of everything that mattered hereabouts, was similarly inclined to make his purposes quite plain.

MacLeod, like Colum Cille, was the sort of person who, as the Thessalonians once said of St Paul, was out to turn the world upside down. But this man of substance is now dead, and he has not been quite so lucky as Columba in his successors. The young people whom you see around the abbey which George MacLeod made such efforts to rebuild seem a cosier crew than either he or Colum Cille would have been prepared to tolerate. The self-satisfied singing and clapping and hand-holding that passes for Christianity in such quarters would not have cut much ice with the Picts or the Northumbrians. And maybe something just a little bit more muscular is needed still.

I had met nobody on my three-mile walk from Port na Curaich to Dun I. But the road outside the abbey has about it all the bustle of a city street. Iona today is what the travel brochures label one of Scotland's premier visitor attractions. And the single-track road leading to the ferry terminal at Fionnphort sometimes seems to be frequented only by long lines of tourist coaches.

There were no such crowds to witness the interment of Columba. Some time prior to his death, tells Adomnan, a 'certain brother', seeking not so much to curry favour as to pay a proper tribute, remarked that, so great was the abbot's renown, his burial would attract more mourners than had ever been seen before in Alba. The people of Dalriada alone, this man remarked, would come to Iona in such numbers as to 'entirely fill it'. But Columba disagreed. 'None but the monks of my monastery will perform my funeral rites,' he said.

So it proved, continues Adomnan, 'for there arose a storm of wind without rain which blew so violently during the three days and nights of his obsequies that it prevented everyone from crossing the sound.'

Today there is no storm. The northerly breeze is sufficient only to produce an intermittent dapple on the water; a refracted flickering of light on the sandy seabed. Above the constant chugging of the ferry's diesel engines the only sound you catch is that of still more country music being played on the vessel's public address system. A party from the abbey are, inevitably, clinging closely to each other. And two American women, more prosaically, are applying silvery barrier cream to their noses to protect them from the unexpectedly ferocious Hebridean sun. In time, as well as space, the Iona ferry removes me from the world of Colum Cille.

CHAPTER THREE

A couple of swans, their wings creaking audibly in flight, are making for Caolas na h-Airde where the two-mile long inlet of Loch Aline meets the Sound of Mull. Swans, so impressive in the air and so graceful on the water, invariably lose their composure on landing. This pair are no exception. Their clumsy splashing seems all the noisier in the stillness of the early morning. They do not quite regain their characteristic dignity until the ripples caused by their arrival have been smoothed away by the northward-setting tidal current washing through Loch Aline's narrow entrance.

All around are the hills of Morvern. It is the start of summer; the time when, in the West Highlands, the first flush of the deer grass can impart to even the most barren mountain landscape an illusion of fertility. But here the various shades of green have a little bit more depth to them. This is a place that would always have attracted human settlement.

On one side of the channel, where the swans have been joined now by a slowly manoeuvring yacht, are the few houses, the shop and the hotel which constitute the village of Lochaline. Colum Cille, travelling here from Iona, some fifty miles distant, is believed to have established its first place of Christian worship. Not far away is Fiunary where, commencing in the 1770s, the ancestors of George MacLeod, the modern Iona community's father figure, occupied Morvern's Church of Scotland manse for more than a century.

The Vikings, ever in search of a good harbour, would no doubt have been active in the vicinity of Loch Aline. And it was in thirteenth-century Morvern, according to the traditions of Clan Donald, whose progenitor he was, that Somerled, the Hebridean warrior prince whose own lineage was partly Norse and partly Gaelic, first proved himself an outstanding leader of men in the course of a stirring clash with the troops of a king of Norway.

Somerled's descendants were to create the Lordship of the Isles. Eastward from Lochaline, on a promontory jutting towards Mull, are the squat, square ruins of Ardtornish Castle, one of their more substantial strongholds. It was to Ardtornish in 1386 on his being taken ill in Ardgour, a good day's march to the north, that John, Lord of the Isles, was carried by his entourage to die. It was at Ardtornish a quarter of a century later, that another Lord of the Isles began to assemble the army which, in faraway Aberdeenshire, would eventually do battle in an attempt to demonstrate that the lordship was more powerful than the kings of Scots. And it was in the great hall of Ardtornish in the 1460s that yet another Lord of the Isles, quarrelling still with the Scottish monarchy, would seek to strengthen his position by signing a treaty drafted jointly by his clerks and by emissaries sent here to Morvern by Edward IV of England.

But for all that its principal men were – with some justice – prone to think of themselves as on a par with kings, the lordship fell at last. From its fall the fortunes of Clan Donald never quite recovered. Now the MacDonalds, who had provided the Lordship of the Isles with its rulers, were just another of the north of Scotland's many tribal groupings.

As for Morvern, it remained initially with the MacLeans, who had been one of the lordship's subordinate kindreds and whose power was centred on extensive possessions on both the mainland and the island shores of the Sound of Mull. But the MacLean lands, like many of the other territories over which successive Lords of the Isles had so impressively presided in the years of their greatness, passed in time into the grip of the Inveraray Campbells – that ceaselessly politicking family whose name was to become synonymous, in much of the Highlands and Islands, with territorial aggrandisement.

Among the clans they had wholly or partially supplanted – the MacDonalds, the MacLeans and several more – the Campbells were regarded, inevitably, with a dislike that verged on loathing. And the resulting tensions, which were none the less powerful for their having become increasingly entwined with altogether wider religious and political aspirations, were to help fuel the many risings and rebellions which occurred in the Highlands and Islands in the sixteenth, seventeenth and eighteenth centuries.

When, in the summer of 1644, Alasdair MacColla – that spirited, princely youth with the power to rouse thousands, as he was described by a MacDonald bard – came from Ireland to Scotland with the nucleus of the little army which, under the joint leadership of MacColla and the Marquis of Montrose, was to win so many dazzling victories over Scotland's Covenanter government and its Campbell backers, it was here in Morvern that the campaign began. Kinlochaline Castle was taken in a single day by Alasdair's men; its capture being made doubly sweet, no doubt, by the fact that this particular keep, whose ruins are still to be seen to the right of the road that leads from Lochaline in the direction of Ardgour, was garrisoned by Campbells.

MacColla, for all his triumphs, was eventually to fail. So too, a century later, was Prince Charles Edward Stuart who made the West Highlands the starting point for his armed attempt on the crown which his ancestors, in MacColla's time and subsequently, had so casually allowed to slip from their grasp.

If it was still remembered in Morvern that the men of the parish, some three hundred years before, had gone to war more than once with the Stewart kings in whose name Prince Charles had landed in Scotland, there was no one, in the hothouse summer of 1745, with sufficient lack of delicacy to mention such an awkward fact. This being ever the last refuge of lost causes, there were plenty of individuals willing to defy their Campbell lairds and to make the trek – by way of Strontian, Polloch and the shores of Loch Shiel – to the Jacobite rallying point at Glenfinnan; to march, for that matter, from Glenfinnan to Edinburgh, to Derby and, ultimately, to Culloden.

But when, in the aftermath of their final encounter with the Duke of Cumberland's redcoats, there came home, in the spring of 1746, those Morvern men who had not fallen victim to government guns or government bayonets, the defeated rebels were to discover that the Hanoverian régime which they had dared to challenge now had a longer reach than central authority had ever possessed in the years when the Lords of the Isles, by means of their fleets of galleys, had controlled the western seaways.

That March there had sailed into Loch Aline the Royal Navy sloops Princess Anne and Terror. And in view of the wholly ruthless nature of the counter-insurgency policy which had led to this little fleet's dispatch to West Highland waters, the name of the latter ship was especially appropriate. By Westminster politicians who had been frightened half to death by the spectacle of a Highland army camped within a hundred or so miles of London, the captains and the crews of the two vessels had been instructed to demonstrate that there was no room, even in the more inaccessible corners of the recently created United Kingdom of England and Scotland, for people calling themselves

43

Jacobite. The naval party's interpretation of their orders involved their setting fire to 'near four hundred' homes in Morvern.

But such reprisals, it appears, did not entirely stamp out disaffection. Some thirty years later, when Norman MacLeod – that most establishment-minded minister whose altogether more rebellious great-great-grandson was to undertake the reconstruction of the abbey on Iona – was installed in Morvern on the instructions of its Campbell proprietor, the Duke of Argyll, his parishioners, a member of MacLeod's family was afterwards to recall, still retained the 'violent prejudices' which had made them 'Prince Charlie men to the core'.

Norman MacLeod's immediate predecessor, so the story went, had been 'commanded' by Morvern's Jacobites 'not to dare in their presence to pray for King George in church, or they would shoot him dead. He did, nevertheless, pray … but not, we fear, in pure faith. He took a brace of pistols with him to the pulpit and, cocking them before the prayer began, he laid them down before him and, for once at least, offered up his petitions with his eyes open.'

Eighteenth-century Morvern was, in every sense of the term, a wild place: roadless, trackless, mostly lawless, too. Campbell of Airds – the gentleman who served as the Duke of Argyll's factor, or land agent, here in the 1730s – found that he could not successfully collect rents from Morvern's MacLean and Cameron tenants unless he came calling on them in the company of a strongly armed posse. And there were reports from government agents to the effect that Morvern, together with the adjacent parishes of Sunart and Ardgour, was among the 'several districts' in the Highlands and Islands which were almost entirely given over to 'depredations and cow stealing'.

But for all its numerous troubles, this was then a populous locality; a place of many hamlets, many farmsteads. That it is so no longer owes a good deal to Morvern's eventual discovery that there were, after all, worse landlords than the Campbells.

One of these was Patrick Sellar. His name is inextricably connected with the ruthless eviction of hundreds of families from Strathnaver in Sutherland with a view to making way for the enormous sheep farm with which Sellar provided himself in the years around 1814. Sellar, however, was active in Morvern also. Strathnaver had made him a wealthy man, but there he was merely a tenant. In Morvern, which an early nineteenth-century Duke of Argyll was obliged to put on the market to ease a temporary financial difficulty and where Sellar began by acquiring the farm of Acharn in 1838, he aspired to be a landlord on his own account.

Just short of Acharn, some four miles north of Lochaline, the road nowadays branches in two. The left-hand fork leads by way of Loch Arienas and Loch Doire nam Mart to Kinlochteacuis. The alternative route goes by way of Gleann Geal to Kingairloch and Strontian. On neither road will you encounter very much in the way of habitation. Once, in the decade that brought Patrick Sellar to these parts, Morvern had a population well in excess of two thousand. Today a fraction of that number lives here. And Sellar bears some part of the responsibility for modern Morvern's lack of people.

From a spot near Altnachonaich I look out across Gleann Geal. It is after nine o' clock. But even in the steeply slanting sunlight of a summer evening – conditions ideally suited to show up the mound-like traces of long abandoned dwellings – there is little to be seen in the way of evidence that folk ever lived here.

Patrick Sellar, Morvern tradition has it, went so far as to employ a local man – a former tailor, it is said, whose own home he had caused to be swallowed up in one of his sheep farms – to remove and level the walls of each newly emptied house and to cover even its foundations with a neatly cut blanket of turf. Because Sellar, who had once been tried in Inverness on criminal charges arising from his conduct in the course of the Strathnaver evictions, was very sensitive as to the extent to which his name had become publicly associated with enforced depopulation, that story seems to me entirely plausible.

From Gleann Geall I head for Loch Doire nam Mart. Near its south-western corner, in a spot now lost to view beneath the spruce trees of one of the Forestry Commission plantations which are today so much a feature of the Morvern scene, there was once to be found a settlement by the name of Aoineadh Mor. Prior to its clearance in the 1820s by one of Patrick Sellar's predecessors – for Sellar, though he was to contribute substantially to the nineteenth-century transformation of Morvern, certainly did not initiate it – Aoineadh Mor was occupied by more than seventy individuals. One of them, in her old age in Glasgow, was to recall, for the benefit of Norman MacLeod, another of the several ministers belonging to that remarkable clerical dynasty stemming from the manse at Fiunary, the last days and hours of this now vanished Morvern township.

On the morning of the day appointed for the destruction of Aoineadh Mor, MacLeod was told, 'the officers of the law' came early to the place; 'and the shelter of a house, even for one night more, was not to be got.'

All such evictions began with the extinguishing of the fires in the homes that were to be cleared. And because these fires – which had been kept carefully alight, day and night, for generations – were seen as symbolic of a community's continuity, the putting out of them was invariably traumatic. 'The hissing of the fire on the flag of the hearth, as they were drowning it, reached my heart,' said Norman MacLeod's informant.

One can imagine her tone as she continued: 'The aged woman, the mother of my husband, James, was then alive, weak and lame. James carried her on his back in a creel. I followed him with little John, an infant, at my breast … I thought my heart would rend. I would feel right if my tears would flow; but no relief thus did I find.'

On the ridge which separates Loch Doire nam Mart from Loch Arienas, the refugee party stopped to take one last look at Aoineadh Mor. 'The houses were being already stripped. The bleat of the big sheep was on the mountain. The whistle of the Lowland shepherd and the bark of his dogs were on the brae.'

These words – spoken originally, of course, in Gaelic – were taken down by Norman MacLeod in the city tenement where this family had finally settled. Some forty years had passed since their removal from Morvern, but in this account of the Aoineadh Mor clearance there was understandable bitterness still. And much of that bitterness was directed, naturally enough, against the shepherd whose single dwelling had taken the place of the many homes which were no more. *Sasunnach*, English, she called this Lowlander, by way of insult. 'It was there that the friendly neighbourhood was,' said Norman MacLeod's Glasgow parishioner of her birthplace, 'though now only one smoke is to be seen, from the house of the Sasunnach shepherd.'

The story of the Aoineadh Mor evictions, as recorded by Norman MacLeod, was published in English in the early 1860s. And no mention was made, either by MacLeod or by the old lady whose memories he thus preserved, of the identity of the man then occupying the shepherd's cottage which figured so prominently in the printed account of Aoineadh Mor's destruction.

That man was called James Dempster. He was my great-grandfather. And the cottage built for him by his employers still stands within a few hundred yards of the spot where, on the morning of their departure, the Aoineadh Mor people paused for their last look at their place.

When sheep-farming was introduced to the Highlands and Islands by those nineteenth-century landowners who were responsible for so many episodes of the Aoineadh Mor sort, it was necessary to import the Blackface and Cheviot flocks on which the new industry was based. The principal sources of supply were those parts of Scotland – most notably the Borders, Dumfries-shire and

Galloway – where this type of agriculture was already securely established. And with the sheep came shepherds: men with skills which few Highlanders then possessed; men who knew how to work the dogs which alone make it possible to manage sheep in hill country; men who could lamb, gather, shear and otherwise take care of the hundreds, even thousands, of valuable animals placed in their charge.

The Dempsters were such men. They came north in the 1830s when my great-great-grandfather, David Dempster, a Dumfries-shire man who had previously been employed on a farm in Ayrshire, took a job as a shepherd in Gleann na h-Iubraich which runs north-eastward from Polloch on the shores of Loch Shiel.

To reach Polloch today you take one of Scotland's more impressive mountain roads which, in the course of rather less than eight miles, both climbs and descends more than a thousand feet by way of a series of hairpin bends of the kind more normally associated with the Alpine countries than with Britain. On your left, as the Polloch road ascends steeply out of Strontian, are the remnants of the lead mines which flourished here in the eighteenth century. In those mines there was discovered the metallic element to which Strontian gave its name and which, in the form strontium-90, is one of the more lethal by-products of the manufacture of nuclear weapons. And to those mines there came the English miners – Kirsops and the like – whose surnames, like those of the Dempsters and other Lowland shepherds of a slightly later period, still linger here and there in this part of the West Highlands.

Strontian, in the 1730s and 1740s, when its lead deposits first began to be exploited, had something of the character of those mining settlements which were to explode into frenzied life in places like California, the Yukon and Australia in the course of the following century. The place was famed for its drunkenness, its thievings, its horse stealings, its banditry, its prostitutes and, inevitably, its gonorrhoea – all of which makes it a little more understandable that one of its eighteenth-century clerics, Daniel MacLachlan, should have been expelled from the Church of Scotland following the publication in London of his most enticingly entitled *Essay upon Improving and Adding to the Strength of Great Britain and Ireland by Fornication*.

An earlier, and altogether more respectable, Strontian minister was Alexander MacDonald who, towards the end of the seventeenth century, was put in charge of an enormous parish which included all of Ardnamurchan, Sunart, Moidart, Arisaig and Morar. MacDonald, who could trace his descent from the Lords of the Isles and who was closely connected with the strongly Jacobite-

ABANDONED ROCK CORES AT STRONTIAN

inclined chiefs of Clanranald, was one of many Highland clergy who refused to take the oaths demanded of all Scottish churchmen following the revolution of 1688. That upheaval resulted in the deposing of the country's last Stuart king, James VII, and made Scotland an avowedly Presbyterian state. But Alexander MacDonald, an Episcopalian as well as a Jacobite, was having none of it. And so entrenched was he among his parishioners that, for all his openly expressed rejection of both the politics and the religion of Scotland's new rulers, he was left in undisturbed occupation of his manse at Dalilea on the Moidart shore of Loch Shiel, some three or four miles, as the crow flies, from Polloch.

In the Gaelic that was the universal speech of these parts in his day, the Revd MacDonald was *Maighstir Alasdair*, Master Alexander. That made his son, also Alexander, *Alasdair mac Mhaighstir Alasdair*. And it is by this name that the younger MacDonald – who was to serve as a commissioned officer in the Jacobite army during the rising of 1745 – is still renowned as one of the foremost Gaelic poets of all time.

From the Forestry Commission viewpoint at Ceanna Garbh, high above the narrow creek formed by the mouth of the Polloch River, the few casual tourists who venture into this nowadays empty quarter look across Loch Shiel to the wood of Coille Druim an Laoigh where Alasdair MacMhaighstir Alasdair once herded his father's cattle. Nearby is Eilean Fhianain, the little island which bears the name of the Columban monk who chose it for his habitation and whose reputation for sanctity was so enduring as to ensure that it still serves occasionally as a burial ground.

MacMhaighstir Alasdair, who grew up within sight of Eilean Fhianain and who is himself buried there, refers to it in his striking evocation of a voyage made to Ireland in *Birlinn Chlann Raghnaill*, Clanranald's Galley. The birlinn's slim, smooth oars – which the vessel's crew slide thankfully into the sea at the end of a storm which has come close to overwhelming them – were cut, the poet says, by one MacVarish from pines growing in the vicinity of Eilean Fhianain.

There are pines still beside Loch Shiel. There is the occasional oak also – possibly descended, if you are of a mind to think of trees in that way, from the oaks that Columba himself came here to fell when in search of suitable roof beams for the monastery church on Iona.

Centuries after Colum Cille's time, islanders were still voyaging to Loch Shiel on similar quests. The River Shiel – which exits from the loch at Acharacle and which flows into the sea, some two or three miles distant, just below the Clanranald stronghold of Caisteal Tioram – was traditionally considered navigable. 'Open boats from the Western Isles are in the practice of entering the lake by the river,' an Ardnamurchan minister reported in the eighteenth century, 'and taking away ladings of the timber on its banks.'

Nor did these boats come empty to Loch Shiel. Cattle from the Uists were sometimes landed at Polloch and driven across the hill for sale at Strontian – one of the localities frequented each September by dealers and drovers who, having purchased the beasts brought there by the islesmen, would drive those animals on by way of Glen Tarbert, the Corran ferry and Glencoe, to the great trysts, or fairs, which were held then every autumn in the Lowland towns of Crieff and Falkirk.

There is no such activity to be observed now from Ceanna Garbh. Here, as in Morvern, there are far fewer people than there were two hundred years ago. From the Moidart side of Loch Shiel, opposite Polloch, MacDonald of Glenaladale took 150 men to serve in Clanranald's regiment at Culloden. And where there were 150 fighting men to be got, there must have been a total population of several hundred. But today there is no human habitation on the north shore of Loch Shiel in all the twenty miles between Dalilea and Glenfinnan. Gleann na h-Iubraich, too, had been emptied of its original occupants before my great-great-grandfather came here. In the glen and those adjoining it – places capable then of carrying several thousand sheep – the census-takers of 1841 found no one with a Highland name; only Browns, Todds and, of course, Dempsters.

David Dempster's wife, Elizabeth, was some years younger than himself. They had met and married in the south. Some at least of their eleven children, including James, my great-grandfather, had been born before the family left Cumnock for the home they were to occupy for much of the remainder of the nineteenth century in Gleann na h-Iubraich. And it is difficult to believe on visiting that home that Elizabeth Dempster, on getting her first sight of it, felt anything other than a profound longing for the much more thickly populated countryside of Ayrshire.

From the head of Loch Doilet – the point, itself a couple of miles inland from Polloch and Loch Shiel, where the public road gets closest to the spot where David Dempster was to live for fifty years or more – I walk into Gleann na h-Iubraich on a day of stiff south-easterly wind and spitting rain. The glen was long since purchased by the Forestry Commission. The sheep which displaced its people have themselves been displaced by stand after stand of conifers. And the place would be as unrecognisable now to its nineteenth-

LOCH SHIEL FROM GLENFINNAN

century shepherds as it would be to the Gaelic-speaking folk who inhabited it before them and who are commemorated today only in the names they gave to its hills, its streams and all its other natural features.

From the house in Gleann na h-Iubraich – a house that is empty and abandoned, its windows broken, its fireplaces piled high with soot and debris from its crumbling chimneys, its floors strewn with the discarded beer cans left by the casual visitors who have camped out in its rooms – I identify various surrounding landmarks with the help of an Ordnance Survey map.

Gleann na h-Iubraich itself leads still further into hills that stretch northwards and eastwards in the direction of Ardgour and Loch Linnhe. Creag Bhreac is on its right, the ridge of Carn Dearg on its left. Directly opposite is Leitir Dubh, which I translate as the dark slope. That the spot was so named, I deduce, owes something to the fact that its northerly aspect is so nearly sheer as to deprive it entirely of sunlight for much of the winter.

Once there were birch trees growing on Leitir Dubh. But they have long since been supplanted by the all-conquering sitka spruce. Only on the hillside's highest reaches, beyond the point at which it made commercial sense for the Forestry Commission to plant its exotic seedlings, are there to be glimpsed the birchwood's thin and straggling remnants.

I walk a little futher up the glen. Whole sections of the forest have been felled here. The ground is strewn with white and weathered logs which, for some reason, were not thought worth extracting. Branches, bark and other fragments have been piled into ungainly heaps with the help of a bulldozer. The scene is utterly depressing.

Not far away is the little river which flows out of Gleann na h-Iubraich in the direction of Loch Doilet, Polloch and Loch Shiel. One of the more adverse environmental effects of intensive afforestation, claim the many critics of the Forestry Commission and its private sector counterparts, is to be found in the fact that conifer plantations so acidify adjacent water courses as to kill the trout which normally flourish in hill burns of this sort. I make my way along the stream's bank for a hundred yards or more. There are no fish to be seen.

At the back of the Gleann na h-Iubraich shepherd's house is a hill park which is surrounded by a dry-stane dyke built neatly in the south country manner and still resisting successive winter storms. Here David Dempster would have folded his sheep at those times of year when they were brought in from the surrounding hills for clipping and the like. Now the park is as unused as the home beside it. I glimpse two red deer hinds watching me from its north-eastern corner. I lift an arm and, alarmed by this sudden movement, the hinds clear the dyke and disappear among the trees which lap its outer edge.

He was a big man, this David Dempster. So I am told by Donald Lawrie from whom I have most of my information about him. Donald was for many years Lochaline's postmaster. He is a very keen local historian and, like me, one of David Dempster's descendants. The descent, in Donald's case, is by way of one of David Dempster's daughters who, Donald informs me, was remembered in his family as talking habitually in Broad Scots which, though common enough in the Dempster country of Ayrshire and Dumfries-shire, would have sounded more than slightly foreign in the Gaelic Highlands.

'The old folk spoke of him as always wearing the heavy tweed plaid of the Borders shepherd and carrying a crook with an iron head to it,' Donald says of David Dempster. 'He was strong, too, very strong. He was in the habit of walking into Strontian for his supplies and then walking back across the hill there with a boll of meal – that's two clear stone over the hundredweight – strapped somehow to his back.'

David Dempster's gravestone in Strontian's churchyard gives his age, at the time of his death in 1901, as exactly one hundred. But Donald Lawrie believes him to have been even older. 'He didn't know exactly when he was born,' Donald says, 'and that's the truth. But the one thing he knew for sure about his age was that he was a shepherd with his own hirsel (the ground occupied by a stock of sheep), in Dumfries-shire somewhere, when the troops came home from Waterloo. Now, if he was a hundred in 1901, he would have been only fourteen when the Battle of Waterloo was fought. And I don't think a boy of fourteen would have been given sole charge of a place. So I'd put the year of his birth around 1796 or 1797.'

At Kinlochan, where I left my car on the morning I came to Gleann na h-Iubraich, is the little croft which David Dempster occupied when he became, at last, too old to be still shepherding. One day at Kinlochan – or so there runs a family tale told yet by my mother – there came calling one of David Dempster's many acquaintances. The visitor, on seeing an obviously elderly individual sunning himself on a bench outside the Kinlochan croft house, began complimenting the old fellow on his evident good health. Not recognising the caller, the seated man was clearly puzzled by his familiarity. Then realisation dawned. 'It's not me you want at all,' said this near eighty-year old, getting spryly to his feet. 'It's my father. He's down the croft there, scything hay!'

When, in the early 1860s, David Dempster's son, James, took on the responsibility for the sheep flock that had then been established for the better part of half a century on the hirsel created by the clearance of Aoineadh Mor, Highland sheep-farming was embarking on its most financially buoyant period. Within twenty years, however, the good times were at an end. Wool had begun to be imported from Australia. With the introduction of refrigerated cargo ships in the 1880s, cheap overseas mutton was quickly to follow. Not until the commencement of state subsidy in the course of the Second World War were sheep producers in the north of Scotland to do well again.

As the nineteenth century wore on and as prospects for sheep steadily deteriorated, James Dempster's employers – whose name was Smith and who had bought, from Patrick Sellar's heirs, the estate to which Sellar, having added greatly to his original purchases in the vicinity of Acharn, had given the ancient title of Ardtornish – were to react in the manner of most Highlands and Islands landlords of the time. Sheep were downgraded in importance. More value was attached now to a property's sporting potential; to its suitability for stalking, in particular. So the Ardtornish Estate, which Patrick Sellar had

DONALD LAWRIE, LOCHALINE

turned over totally to sheep, began to be converted gradually into a deer forest.

Between Patrick Sellar and his successors at Ardtornish there was little similarity. Sellar made his fortune from land management. The still greater wealth which Octavius Smith was deploying in Morvern at the time James Dempster became one of his shepherds had very different origins. The Smiths had begun as wholesale grocers in London. Morvern, to them, was a place to spend money, not a place to earn it. Something of that is reflected still in the peculiarly ornate towers of Ardtornish House, the spacious mansion which Octavius Smith provided for himself at the head of Loch Aline.

All Victorian lairds, if only in imitation of the queen's own lavish lifestyle at that most emulated Highland estate, Balmoral, aspired to a home of the Ardtornish type. What was unusual about Octavius Smith is not that he took such care over his own creature comforts; his employees, too, were extremely well housed by the standards of the time.

In the Black Isle, that tract of fertile farmland to the north of Inverness where he very probably went each autumn with his proportion of the younger sheep which West Highland flockmasters were obliged to overwinter in such comparatively sheltered locations, James Dempster had met and courted Ann MacDonald. The couple were married there in the early summer of 1861. On their return to Morvern they moved into the home which Octavius Smith had provided for them at a spot to which the estate management – and, following them, the Ordnance Survey mapmakers – now gave the anglicised name of Durinemast.

Standing on slightly rising ground at the western end of Loch Arienas, the Durinemast shepherd's cottage – nowadays occupied once more by a family after a long spell as one of those holiday homes so irritatingly prevalent in Morvern and the rest of the West Highlands – still has about it something of that solidly constructed character which must have been all the more impressive in the 1860s when the typical dwelling in these parts had a thatched roof, rubble-filled walls and a floor of hard-packed earth.

Octavius Smith and his son Valentine, who inherited Ardtornish Estate on his father's death in 1871, were eventually to build some thirty such houses for their workforce. And by the 1890s that workforce, by modern standards, was astonishingly large. It totalled nearly forty, among them shepherds, ploughmen, foresters, farm girls and farm labourers, a smith, a carpenter, a coachman and – with the steady expansion of the area given over to deer stalking – a growing number of gamekeepers and ghillies.

Among the latter was a young man from Strontian named John Cameron. Since leaving school in 1885 or thereabouts, he had held a variety of jobs, including a stint as the driver of the pony and trap which then carried the mail between Strontian and Ardgour. Now, because he was courting James Dempster's younger daughter, Catherine, John Cameron was looking to settle down and get a home for himself. This he accomplished just after the turn of the century by moving from Ardtornish to the neighbouring property of Kingairloch.

Once, like Ardtornish, Kingairloch had been held by the MacLeans. Now, also like Ardtornish, it was largely a sporting estate and as such had recently been purchased by a wealthy Derbyshire family by the name of Strutt. But the Strutts, for all that they were primarily interested in Kingairloch's deer stalking attributes, were known also to be looking for a ploughman. John Cameron applied successfully for the position. It brought him a house and an extra two shillings a week. And on the strength of these much improved prospects, he and Catherine Dempster were married in 1904. The couple were to remain in Kingairloch until John's retirement in 1937. I knew them, in their old age, as my grandfather and grandmother.

There have been Camerons in Strontian for a long time. One, Hugh Cameron – who, though of illegitimate birth, was closely related to the leading men of his clan – held lands in Ariundle, some two or three miles upstream from the mouth of the Strontian River, in the 1670s. Other Strontian Camerons, in the following century, turn up in various official documents. Some are described as 'wicked and rebellious people', horse thieves and the like. And one, John Cameron by name, is listed – as a 'whiskie maker in Strontian' – among the many prisoners taken by the British army in the course of the last Jacobite rebellion.

Maybe this John Cameron is among my ancestors; maybe not. The earliest Strontian forebear of whom I can be reasonably certain is one more of my great-great-grandfathers, yet another John Cameron, who, in the 1840s, was the tenant of a croft at Anaheilt – where the Polloch road today leaves the rather busier tourist route to Salen and Acharacle.

This John Cameron was born in the early 1790s which, if the two were directly connected, might have made him the grandson of that earlier John Cameron who had been prevailed upon to abandon his Strontian whisky still for the altogether chancier business of enlisting with Prince Charles.

The Anaheilt John Cameron of the 1840s is described in a Strontian Estate rental book of that time as a miller. And the 1841 census gives the age of his son, Allan, as 26. This accords with family tradition – on which one has to rely in such matters for the period prior to the start, in 1855, of the compulsory registration of births – that Allan Cameron, my great-grandfather, was born in the year of the Battle of Waterloo.

Tradition also insists that Allan Cameron was known always in Gaelic as *Ailean an t-Saoir*, meaning literally the joiner's Allan. This was a common enough way of identifying a man by reference to his father or, as in this case, to his father's profession. It signified simply that Allan was the local carpenter's son.

Allan Cameron's Gaelic designation, then, suggests that John Cameron, Ailean an t-Saoir's father, though entered in the surviving records as a miller, was also a joiner. This is plausible enough. The two trades were often combined. And Allan himself – for all that he was afterwards to earn his living as a stalker – began, as was customary, by following in his father's business. He is described as a capable carpenter in a report made in 1852 to the trustees appointed to manage the affairs of the semi-bankrupt Riddell family who then owned all the extensive territories stretching from Strontian westward to Ardnamurchan Point.

Allan Cameron, by 1852, had taken on the family croft at Anaheilt where he lived with his wife, his mother and his sister. The rent of the place was three pounds fifteen shillings annually. And Allan was then two pounds fifteen shillings in arrears – a performance rated 'good' by the Strontian Estate accountants at a time when, in the aftermath of the widespread famine which had followed the repeated failure of the Highland potato crop in the later 1840s, the Riddells were owed many thousands of pounds by their crofting tenantry.

A common managerial response to such indebtedness was to arrange for the clearance of the crofters concerned. This policy was certainly pursued vigorously on the Riddell lands in the 1850s. Nor was inability to pay the rent a necessary prelude to eviction. A crofter's offence might be simply that his hovel was spoiling the view from his landlord's window. And such, it seems, was the case with Allan Cameron and his neighbours. The crofts at Anaheilt, it was noted in the estate report of 1852, were 'in the immediate neighbourhood of the mansion house and it was agreed last year that, as opportunity offered, the crofters should be removed and the land converted into pasture'.

Whether Allan Cameron was, in fact, evicted I do not know. But at some point in the 1850s he certainly took himself and his family to Ardgour. From there, when she was expecting her fourth child, Allan Cameron's wife set out one winter's day to tramp the thirty or more miles to her mother's home in Ardnamurchan in order to have on hand the help she would need with the imminent birth. In Glen Tarbert, the rocky pass between Ardgour and Strontian, there came on a sudden blizzard of snow. Unable to reach shelter, the pregnant woman died.

Allan Cameron marked with a stone cairn the spot where his wife's body was discovered after the eventual thaw. But the builders of the modern road, not caring that such a monument might be of some modest consequence, swept its rocks into the road's foundations, so where the tragedy occurred exactly there is now no way of finding out.

Allan Cameron married again in 1862. His second wife, Mary, like his first, came from Ardnamurchan; her maiden name was also Cameron. And in 1872 the couple's fourth child John, my mother's father, was born in the two-roomed croft house which the family were then occupying at Clovullin in Ardgour.

Not long afterwards, Allan moved to the Mamore Estate. There – in the vicinity of the place where, some thirty years afterwards, the British Aluminium Company would construct the electrically fuelled smelter which became the focus for the modern town of Kinlochleven – he was employed as a stalker. And it was in that capacity, later in the 1870s, that Allan returned to Strontian and to yet another home, this time at Ariundle.

There hangs on the wall of my own house in Skye a photograph taken at about this time of Ailean an t-Saoir. It shows a whiskered, lean-faced, straight-nosed man. He is wearing a tweed cap and a heavy jacket. If you let your imagination run away with you just a little bit, you might describe his eyes as having that far-sighted look you get about men whose profession depends on their ability to pick out a deer on a distant slope where the rest of us are practically incapable of distinguishing anything by way of detail.

From an old man whose mother was my grandfather's elder sister, I heard some years ago in Strontian of how Allan, who had very little English, was one day accompanying a visiting sportsman into the hills where the glen beyond Ariundle bends eastward towards the high part of Glen Gour. It was raining. And since the ground they were traversing had been stalked the previous afternoon, Allan was not hopeful of success. But then, his jacket wringing wet and his spirits at rock bottom, Allan glimpsed a stag – and a very fine animal at that. He pointed it out to his companion and the two men set out to stalk the beast.

Their route took them, in the still incessant rain, through a succession of boggy mires and peat hags. And it was a very damp and dirty Allan who thus brought his employer's southern guest to the point at which it was possible to get in a shot.

Had he ever killed a stag before, the aspiring sportsman was asked by the soaked and greatly harassed Highlander at his side. 'No,' came the reply.

'Well,' said Allan in his broken English, driving home his message by opening up the knife he used for gralloching, or gutting, deer and drawing its gleaming blade slowly across his throat, 'you had better make sure that you kill this one!'

Allan Cameron's house at Ariundle is in ruins now. Its roof has long gone. Rowan and hawthorn trees grow from its crumbling walls. Bracken swamps the little field where Allan would have cut his hay. But if you go there in spring you will still see in flower the daffodils which someone who once lived here planted in this spot.

The track from Ariundle joins the Polloch road just a mile or so short of Strontian. I follow it southward, taking the route my grandfather took each morning, well over a century ago, when on his way to school. I pass the churchyard where old David Dempster's gravestone stands. I come to the bridge; this was the community's traditional meeting place. On its parapets the men of the place were in the habit of sitting themselves down of an evening, lighting their pipes and debating the public issues of the time.

GLEN TARBERT

It was near this bridge on an August day in 1879 – having been barred from the local school on the orders of Strontian's laird and Allan Cameron's employer, Sir Thomas Riddell – that the veteran land reformer, John Murdoch, conducted one of those impromtu and open-air meetings at which, as always, he called on his audience to begin to campaign actively for those rights which their landlords had so long denied to them. 'I met with a good many people about and heard their complaints,' Murdoch recalled of his Strontian trip. Perhaps coincidentally, perhaps not, the locality was afterwards to become one of the strongholds of the Highland Land League – that most radical organisation which, during the 1880s, forced the government in London to grant to crofters the security of tenure they have ever since enjoyed.

Was the seven-year old John Cameron among the Strontian people who gathered to hear John Murdoch speak, as the latter noted subsequently, 'under a splendid elm tree which sheltered us well from the rain'? Possibly; possibly not.

On the one hand is the fairly self-evident fact that a lad of his age would not have been much interested in the substance of Murdoch's Gaelic address. On the other hand, however, is the equally undeniable circumstance that such a controversial occasion, in a place where excitements of any kind were few and far between, must have possessed its own fascination for the small boys round about.

But whether or not he ever listened to John Murdoch, my grandfather, from whom I first heard of the doings of Patrick Sellar and of the clearance of Aoineadh Mor, would have agreed wholeheartedly with Murdoch's views. John Cameron was assuredly no admirer of landlords.

James Dempster's house at Durinemast is occupied now by the warden of an adjacent nature reserve, managed by the Scottish Wildlife Trust. The ruins of Allan Cameron's home in Ariundle are in the centre of another such reserve, this one owned by Scottish Natural Heritage. Both sites have been so designated because they contain some of the best preserved remnants of the oak forests which once covered so much of this corner of the Highlands. Conservationists, who exercise great influence in the north of Scotland nowadays, are accordingly inclined to make much of their value as places where it is possible to be less aware than usual of mankind's generally all-pervasive impact on our landscape.

I find this a little ironic. To me, for reasons that will be clear enough by now, the primary significance of both Durinemast and Ariundle is the association they have with things human rather than with things natural. But this is not to say, I should take care to emphasise, that I do not welcome the widespread contemporary concern for the well-being of such places. I welcome it very much.

The Ariundle oakwood, as it happens, had its share of management in the past. But its managers – thankfully – had never been in the employ of the Forestry Commission which, not far from here and as recently as the 1960s, actually tried to make a virtue of replacing native oak with sitka.

There were no clear-fells of the Gleann na h-Iubraich type in Ariundle. Instead its trees were carefully cut and coppiced in such a fashion as always to preserve the wood's overall integrity. Ariundle probably provided Strontian's lead miners with their pit props. Its oaks certainly fuelled the charcoal kilns which can still be found here. But for all that the wood was thus exploited, its regenerative capacities were never quite destroyed. And so today, should you decide to go to Ariundle, most preferably on one of those dazzlingly sunny mornings we tend to get in the West Highlands in the early part of summer, you can be fairly confident that the trees you will see around you – not just oaks but several other species such as birch and holly – have been following on their predecessors, generation after generation, since the wood itself first began to take shape in the aftermath of the last Ice Age.

There is much deserving of being safeguarded in a place like Ariundle; more, perhaps, than Scottish Natural Heritage, which tends to think in strictly scientific terms, has yet got round to incorporating in its plans.

'They worship the gods without making use of temples,' a Roman author recorded of the Celts of Gaul. Their most sacred places, wrote another Roman of those fierce and fiery warriors, were invariably 'groves of oak'.

So it was also among the pagan Celts of the British Isles. And it is not, I think, too fanciful to discern something of these ancient affinities enduring in the outlook of the Christian successors to the druid priests of earlier times.

There were two spots in Ireland which Colum Cille is thought to have regarded with particular favour: one was Derry, one was Durrow. Both these modern placenames are corruptions of the Gaelic word applied still to an oak tree.

Nor did the Columban Church ever try, in the manner of those Continental clerics who so clearly felt themselves to be the inheritors of the temple-building traditions of the Romans and the Greeks, to honour God in great cathedrals. Its monks preferred to seek their inspiration in those places – of which Iona was one and Skellig Michael off the coast of Kerry another – where the divine purpose seemed almost as likely to be revealed in the roar of the wind and the glint of the sea as it was to be found in the holy books so laboriously copied in the monastery scriptorium.

Scribbled here and there on manuscripts which were penned some twelve or thirteen centuries ago, one finds still hints as to how the Gaelic-speaking churchmen of Columba's time thought about their world. That world, as I have already suggested, did not seem to them a dismal vale of tears. It was a place where a blackbird – which the monastic scribe who made this remark described carefully as the possessor of a bright yellow beak and a distinctive whistle – could be likened playfully to a hermit needing no bell to ward off strangers. It was a place where, almost in the manner of a modern naturalist, a man might comment perceptively on the detailed doings of the bees to be seen from the open door of his stone cubicle. It was a place, above all, to be enjoyed, to be appreciated. 'Pleasant is the glittering of the sun today upon those margins,' wrote another monk in the course of the long gone epochs which English historians would one day entitle the Dark Ages, 'because it shimmers so.'

The eighth-century Gael who longed to have 'a secret hut in the wilds' with 'a lovely wood around it on every side to nurse the singing birds' would, without doubt, have warmed to Ariundle.

So would Alasdair MacMhaighstir Alasdair who, a whole millenium later, must have passed this way on his frequent journeyings through Ardnamurchan and Sunart. MacMhaighstir Alasdair, like his monastic predecessors and like that other great eighteenth-century Gaelic poet, *Donnchadh Ban Mac an t-Saoir*, Duncan MacIntyre, wrote of nature not – in the manner of Wordsworth and the Romantics – as something to moralise about but, rather, as something of which he and people generally were, in a matter of fact sort of fashion, an integral and inseparable component.

There is no preaching in MacMhaighstir Alasdair's lyrical accounts of the passing seasons. Neither is there any sentimentality in Donnchadh Ban's descriptions of the deer he encountered during his career as a stalker on the hills between Tyndrum and Bridge of Orchy. But what is to be found in large measure, in the work of both those Highland poets, is a wealth of observation and insight of a kind that serves to demonstrate the extent to which a profound awareness of the natural world has forever been a vital element in the Gaelic consciousness.

I do not mind greatly when folk from elsewhere tell me, as they do from time to time, that Highlanders ought to be grateful for the beauty of their surroundings. That can be construed – in one's more charitable moments at any rate – as one of those slightly fumbled, but essentially well-meaning, comments made by guests who, without knowing quite how to go about it, think they should be paying a suitable compliment to a locality which they have felt privileged to visit.

What I do resent is any implication that Highlanders need to be taught by others how to appreciate the Highlands. For close on fifteen hundred years now, ever since the reciters of the Ulster sagas – drawing, perhaps, in Ireland on their knowledge of the Dalriada settlements – caused Deirdre to lament so eloquently her departure from her Scottish glen of steep-ridged peaks and pools and dappled deer and rowans and hawks and round-faced otters, our literature has consisted very largely of our efforts to explore the meaning of our place.

CHAPTER FOUR

When, on Dunadd being first pointed out to me as a small boy, I was told it had once been the capital of Scotland, I treated this information with a good deal of private reserve. National capitals were places like Washington, Paris, London or – in some peculiarly subordinate sense which I could not then quite figure out – Edinburgh. National capitals were conglomerations of imposing buildings: houses of parliament, royal palaces, great castles and the like. National capitals contained a country's rulers: its kings, its queens, its princes and princesses. The notion that such people might ever have had any but the most transient connection with this little hill, some four or five miles from Lochgilphead in the middle district of Argyll, seemed to me to be quite unbelievable.

But I was wrong. Dunadd, for something like three hundred years, was one of the principal strongholds of Dalriada. Here, prior to such ceremonies being removed to Iona, some at least of the leading men of that Gaelic-speaking realm went through the rites which made them kings. And since Dalriada, while only one small part of the country we call Scotland, was then the most important part of that country to be occupied and governed by Scots, there is indeed a sense in which Dunadd, for all my youthful scepticism, can plausibly be argued to have been for a time our nation's central place.

Returning here, not long after dawn on a September Saturday, I find little recognition of that fact. The approach to the hill is by way of a farm track which, this morning, is spattered liberally with puddles. There was heavy rain

LOCH GARRY

IONA CATHEDRAL FROM DUN I

RUIN IN KNOYDART

FISHERMAN'S HUT, BENBECULA

HEAVILY POPULATED RURAL SETTLEMENT IN LEWIS. THE VILLAGE OF CROSS IN NESS

BURN, SUTHERLAND

THE 'ROUGH BOUNDS' FROM ABOVE LOCH GARRY

THE CUILLIN HILLS AND LOCH SCAVAIG FROM ELGOL

CELTIC CROSS, IONA

CROSSES IN CILLE CHOIRIL, ROY BRIDGE

CHURCH AT LOCHAILORT

in the night. Now the wind has veered into the north-west and the sky has begun to clear, but the sun is still below the horizon and the morning feels unseasonably cold. The clouds have about them something of that yellowish tinge which, in winter, warns of the imminence of sleet or hail. It would not be surprising if there were to be a coating of snow on the high tops before the day is out.

A hump-backed bridge crosses the River Add beside the farm to which the track gives access. The water below is dark and slow-flowing. The sea is nearly three miles distant. But the land here is flat and low-lying, so the river has none of that noisy briskness which is so characteristic of most West Highland streams.

The extent of the plain surrounding the hill goes some way towards explaining its occasionally pivotal role in the Dalriadan scheme of things. In the hours of daylight at any rate, no hostile force could have approached Dunadd while remaining undetected by its garrison. Any attack on that garrison would have had to be mounted from dangerously exposed positions. Should the attackers have succeeded in reaching the hill's base, they would have faced further hazards; Dunadd's rocky slopes are so steep as to be nearly sheer. In addition, its sixth- and seventh-century occupants reinforced the hill's natural defences with a series of concentric walls and ramparts, the remnants of which are still to be seen as you climb towards the summit.

Dunadd was one of the military keys to Dalriada. The hill commanded – as it still commands – the narrow isthmus between the Sound of Jura and Loch Fyne. It would consequently have been impossible for any hostile force – such as might have been expected, at certain periods, to march out of Pictland – to advance into the Dalriadan heartlands of Knapdale and Kintyre without first subduing this most formidable of strongpoints. It is not unnatural, then, given Dunadd's immense strategic significance, that the Gaelic-speaking people who moved to this part of Argyll from Antrim should have chosen to crown their monarchs here. A few relics of their coronation rituals are still to be seen. The shape of a boar is engraved on a rock. On the same rock are a few lines of the script known as ogham, the linear alphabet first devised in fourth-century Ireland. No modern scholar has been able to decipher this inscription. Nor can anyone now be certain of the precise function of the nearby ewer which was long ago hollowed from the smooth surface of a grey stone outcrop just below Dunadd's highest point.

But the foot-shaped incision immediately adjacent to the ogham markings is an altogether different proposition. Its purpose is clear enough from descriptions of the ways in which much later Gaels, both in the Scottish Highlands and in Ireland, marked an important individual's formal assumption of his powers and his inheritance.

Hoping that no one is witnessing such foolishness, I remove both the boot and sock from my right foot. The water in the footprint marking is icy to the touch. It is made the more unpleasant by its having been discoloured by the dung left by a cow which must somehow have broken through the fence now separating Dunadd from the surrounding fields. But at least my foot, which is a smallish 8½, fits neatly into the space provided for it by a craftsman of some fifteen centuries ago. It is impossible to be certain, of course. But it seems likely that I have just repeated – a little impiously, perhaps – one part of the ceremonial surrounding the inauguration of a Dalriadan king.

Dark Age mumbo-jumbo? Possibly. But when, in 1953, the United Kingdom of Great Britain and Northern Ireland crowned its present queen – whose own claim to her throne depends, in part at least, on her descent from the royal families of Dalriada – her advisers took great care to have her seated, in Westminster Abbey, on a slab of rock which derives such mystical significance as it may possess from its role in ancient Gaelic ritual of the kind conducted on Dunadd.

The Stone of Destiny, on which kings of Scots had been crowned from time immemorial and which was believed traditionally to have been brought from Ireland to Dalriada by some of the earliest emigrants from Ulster, was looted from Scone some seven hundred years ago by Edward I of England. It has been kept in London ever since; except, of course, for the few weeks it spent again in Scotland following its removal from Westminster in December 1950 by a group of Glasgow students. And it is indicative of the emotions still surrounding this particular totem – which looks outwardly to be the last place you would expect a modern queen to park her backside at the moment of her coronation – that the young Scots who brought it north, on that occasion, were pursued with all the vigour of which the British state is capable.

The Stone of Destiny left Argyll in the middle years of the ninth century when a Dalriadan monarch succeeded in imposing his rule over Picts as well as Scots. This king's Gaelic name has long been anglicised as Kenneth MacAlpin. Although the state he created did not yet incorporate lands lying to the south of the Firths of Forth and Clyde, his kingdom – soon to bear the Latin designation Scotia – was much more evidently the nucleus of modern Scotland than Dalriada, by itself, had ever been.

The Gaels today have been for so long culturally beleaguered, with their very language hovering currently on the borders of extinction, that it is extraordinarily hard for us to comprehend and visualise the distant time when Gaelic-speaking kings and noblemen were able to bend others to their will. But the astonishingly rapid demise of both the Picts and Pictish is eloquent testimony to the extent of the Dalriadan supremacy. The Pictish form of speech is irretrievable; and of this previously powerful people, who had been in Alba far longer than the Gaels, there survive now only the ruins of their brochs, or fortresses, and – scattered through the fields of northern and eastern Scotland – the stone pillars on which successive Pictish priests or craftsmen carved the religious and other symbols of their race.

For at least a dozen generations the boundary between Dalriada and the country of the Picts had run somewhere down the mountain chain which now separates Argyll from Perthshire. And there can be no doubt as to which of the two – occasionally feuding – nations had derived the greater benefit from that territorial arrangement.

Argyll, as can be seen from Dunadd and as becomes all the clearer when one drives on south by way of Tarbert into the Kintyre peninsula, is not without its share of fertile farmland. But there is nothing here to compare with the Pictish heartlands to the east; with the Black Isle and with the Moray coast; with the lower-lying parts of Aberdeenshire; with the Howe of the Mearns and the Carse of Gowrie; with Strathmore and with Angus and with Fife. These localities now contain some of this country's most attractive farms and the contrast between such places and the much less productive mountain country to the west would have no less evident to the men of Dalriada than it is to Highlanders today.

Heading towards the Lowlands, through Aviemore, Dalwhinnie and the high pass of Drumochter, on one of those raw April mornings when there is more than a sprinkling of new snow on the Cairngorms, I become aware – as always – on dropping down into Glen Garry and approaching Blair Atholl that I am entering a much more hospitable landscape than the one through which I have been travelling since leaving the Atlantic coast: livestock in this quarter have a less bedraggled look; the grass and trees are lusher; the season much further advanced. The weather here is more reliable, the harvests more substantial and predictable than in the chancier, damper climate which has always been so characteristic of the parts of Scotland where the Gaels first chose to settle.

Beyond Blair Atholl are Pitlochry and Dunkeld. Still further south, on a road which was regularly contested by rebel Highland armies in centuries when it was less profitable to be a Gael than it had been at the time when Kenneth MacAlpin was beginning to exercise his political authority in this vicinity, is

Scone. Here, at the point where the waters of the Tay start to be tidal, those Gaelic-speaking monarchs who had now made themselves the masters of the larger part of Alba, established their latest capital – and the new home of their Stone of Destiny – at the strategic centre of the former Pictish realms.

The fate which now befell the Picts was not dissimilar to that which was one day to overtake their conquerors. As English was to become the key to advancement in the nineteenth and twentieth-century Highlands, so Gaelic was the prestige medium of communication in ninth and tenth-century Pictland; it was the language of the court, the language of the Church, the language of the people in control. Here and there, no doubt, a Pict was forcibly deprived of his possessions – and maybe even killed – by those Gaels who followed their kings eastwards. But the Picts, for the most part, were probably assimilated rather than exterminated, their cultural and linguistic identity submerged in that of the new ruling order.

Soon modern Fife and Angus, Perthshire, Kincardineshire, Aberdeenshire, Banffshire, Moray and Nairn had become wholly Gaelic-speaking. That is why – though it is a part of Scotland which, as a result of subsequent developments, seems to us to have no great amount in common with the Highlands – many of that area's placenames are still so clearly Gaelic. That is how it came about that the earliest surviving lines of Gaelic which we know for certain to have been set down in Scotland, by Scots, were written, many miles to the east of the Highlands, in a place where Gaelic has not been heard now for six or seven hundred years.

The Gaelic passages in question, which show the beginnings of the modern differentiation between the Gaelic dialects of Scotland and of Ireland, were inscribed in their gospel book by the monks of the monastery of Deer in Buchan. Today, and for a long time past, the folk of that eastward-jutting promontory, its coastline running from Kinnaird Head to the estuary of the Ythan, have been famed much more for their command of the language we call Scots than they have been known for their familiarity with Gaelic.

But the balance of such things was radically different in the past. To the compilers of those jottings in that Aberdeenshire gospel book, after all, the Hebrides – which seem to us to be the focus of most things to do with Gaelic – might well have been known, if they were known at all, as *Inse Gall*. That Gaelic phrase can be most handily translated as the islands of the foreigners. And such a designation was appropriate; for, at the time the monks of Deer were ensuring their modest posthumous renown as the country's earliest Gaelic authors, the Hebrides did not belong to Scotland.

For all that their composers have been dead now for a thousand years, there is still to be discerned in the verses made by the likes of Egil Skalla Grimsson and Bjorn Cripplehand something of the sheer delight which the Vikings took in their terrorising of the Gaels. His king, whom he entitles 'the destroyer of the Scots', is described by Egil as feeding the wild animals on corpses, providing dinner for the eagles and enabling the wolves to tear hungrily at the exposed flesh of the wounded. Bjorn's poetry deals equally in slaughter, in 'the house-destroying fire' which the Norsemen bring to Lewis, in the life lost to their swordblades in the Uists, in the blood they freely shed in Skye, Tiree and Mull, and in the smoke that rises over Islay as they sail, in triumph, southward to the Isle of Man and Ireland.

'Bitter is the wind tonight,' wrote one Gaelic-speaking monk in the course of the centuries which the Vikings made their own. 'It tosses the white hair of the ocean. Tonight I fear not the fierce warriors from Norway.'

But even the most powerful storm offered only temporary protection. Each spring still in the Hebrides the wind tends to blow, much more than at other

CROFTER AT KENMORE BY SHIELDAIG, WESTER ROSS

times of year, from the north and from the east. The sky is often clear then and the days are quickly lengthening. This was the season when, for decade after decade, the Viking raiders launched their longships in the Norwegian fiords and, taking advantage of those highly favourable breezes, sailed quickly west and south by way of Shetland, Orkney and the Minch.

They came first to the Hebrides towards the end of the eighth century when the chronicle which the Gaels kept in the north of Ireland makes mention of the 'devastating of all the islands of Britain by the gentiles'. They returned, as the *Ulster Annals* gloomily record, year after year thereafter.

From the writings of Walafrid Strabo – a ninth-century abbot of Reichenau in Bavaria and a man who got his information from itinerant Irish monks of the kind who were commonly to be found then in that part of the Continent – it is possible to get some impression of the Viking impact on the Gaelic world; most specifically on the community which Colum Cille had long before established on Iona.

It was there in 825, according to the Ulster annalists, that one Blathmac was martyred in the course of his attempt to protect the shrine of Columba himself from Norwegian marauders. And it is this event which, in his distant German monastery, Walafrid Strabo set out to draw to the attention of a wider European audience. Warned of impending attack, says Walafrid, Blathmac had determined to stand firm and unyielding against the 'pagan horde'. So committed was he to maintaining the monastic routine, Walafrid goes on, that Blathmac was in the very act of celebrating mass when 'the violent and cursed host came rushing through the open buildings, threatening cruel perils to the blessed men. And after slaying with mad savagery the rest of the brethren, they approached the holy father to compel him to give up the precious metals wherein lie the bones of St Columba.'

But the Iona monks, on Blathmac's instructions, had earlier 'lifted the shrine from its pediments and placed it in the earth, in a hollowed barrow, under a thin layer of turf.' Though the Norsemen, Walafrid continues, greatly desired to have this booty, Blathmac was equally of a mind that they were not on any account to be allowed to disturb the bones of the Iona abbey's founder. So Iona's champion remained, says Walafrid, 'with unarmed hand' but 'with unshaken purpose' until the Vikings, at last, killed him where he stood.

It was after this gory episode that certain relics of Colum Cille were carried to Dunkeld in Perthshire – now emerging as the centre of Kenneth MacAlpin's new, more powerful, Scottish state. It was also at this time, in all probability, that there was taken from Iona to County Meath – and thus to that other Columban monastery from which it derives its name – the lavishly illuminated manuscript which, under the title of the *Book of Kells*, can now be seen in the library of Trinity College, Dublin, where it is one of the more famous of the modern Irish Republic's many visitor attractions.

But soon the Norsemen – the last of Western Europe's barbarian invaders – came to settle in the Hebrides as well as to harry and to steal. Converted now to the faith of the martyred Blathmac and other worshippers of the 'white Christ', whom they had begun by regarding as self-evidently inferior to their own more manly and more warlike gods, the Vikings mingled more and more with Gaels. Marriages between the two peoples became common. Whole families from the Scottish islands voyaged on Norse longships to Norway and to Denmark, as well as to Faroe, Iceland and those other Viking settlements which lay still further to the west. Thus it came about that when Thorfin Karlsevni, in 1010 or thereabouts, anchored his weatherbeaten vessel off a previously unknown coast in what may well have been modern Nova Scotia, the two members of his crew whom Thorfin sent ashore to make an initial exploration of these lands – where, eight hundred years later, so many Scottish Highlanders would seek refuge from the clearances – were men whose place of birth was in the Hebrides.

The Norse influence on Gaelic Scotland lingers still. Many modern Highlanders have Viking personal names. Hebridean blood groups, medical research has demonstrated, are similar to those prevailing in the north and west of Norway. Of the hundred or so crofting townships in twentieth-century Lewis, which is one of the most solidly Gaelic-speaking localities in contemporary Scotland, around four-fifths have names which are purely Scandinavian. Here – in a district where, on the orders of the Western Isles Council, Gaelic has quite properly taken over from the previously all-prevailing English on the roadside signposts at the entry to each island village – there are, ironically enough, far fewer Gaelic-derived placenames than one finds now in the former Pictish territory of Aberdeenshire.

Many Gaelic words to do with shipping and the sea – the terms for anchors, rudders, boats and all things of that sort – are clearly Norse in origin. The ground-hugging stone cottages in which island crofters lived until comparatively recently were not unlike the dwellings to be found in Norway in the Viking period. And the Norsemen's ships, being sleeker, faster and more seaworthy than any coracle, provided models for those galleys which were to be the source of many a Gaelic-speaking Hebridean chieftain's power in

71

centuries when the Viking presence in these waters had become a distant, semi-legendary memory.

Clanranald's birlinn, as evoked in the eighteenth-century poetry of Alasdair MacMhaighstir Alasdair, is the readily recognisable descendant of the long-ships of a thousand years before. Though the galley's crew are overtaken by an especially violent storm in the course of their voyage from the Uists to Ireland, their vessel proves so strongly built as to ensure that the gale is weathered virtually unscathed by the birlinn's crew. When the wind drops at last and the sea becomes smooth again, the Uistmen, utilising skills inherited from their Nordic predecessors, quickly ship their damaged mast, deploy their oars of Eilean Fhianain pine and strike out for shelter on the eastern coast of Antrim.

In an Icelandic saga dealing principally with the affairs of the Norse earldom of Orkney – which was to remain a Norwegian possession until the 1480s and where a variant of Norse was spoken until the eighteenth century – there is to be found a convincingly matter-of-fact portrayal of the leading Viking farmer and freebooter, Svein Asleifarson of Gairsay: 'This is how Svein used to live. Winter he would spend at home on Gairsay where he entertained some eighty men at his own expense. His drinking hall was so big that there was nothing in Orkney to compare with it. In the spring he had more than enough to occupy him, with a great deal of seed to sow which he saw to carefully himself. Then, when that job was done, he would go off plundering in the Hebrides and Ireland on what he called his spring trip; then back home just after midsummer where he stayed till the cornfields had been reaped and the grain was safely gathered in. After that, he would go off raiding again and never came back until the first month of winter was ended.'

The Viking overlords of the Hebrides – to which the Norsemen gave the name of *Sudreyjar*, the Southern Isles, to distinguish the region from the more northerly islands of Orkney and Shetland – very probably conducted themselves, initially at least, in the happily anarchic fashion of Gairsay's Svein Asleifarson. As things began to settle down, however, there emerged from among their number a set of influential and more organised individuals whose rule extended right across an island realm stretching from the Isle of Man, through Islay, Mull and Skye, to Lewis. Though they owed, at times, a loose allegiance to various Scandinavian monarchs, these men were, in practice, independent princes. As such they took, in the course of the tenth century, to referring to themselves as kings, or lords, of the isles. This was a designation of which a great deal more was one day to be heard.

From the ramparts of Edinburgh Castle, on the evening of the day that has taken me south through Perthshire, I look out across the garishly lit modern city. The waters of the Firth of Forth are the same dull grey as battleships. The wind is chill in my face. The distant hills are one-dimensional silhouettes picked out against the quickly fading sunset. The Highlands from this place – the source and symbol, over several centuries, of powerful forces for change of a kind which Highlanders very seldom wanted – seem extremely far away.

In the former royal apartments, not many yards behind me, there was born to Mary Queen of Scots the baby who, as James VI, would become one of Scottish Gaeldom's more implacable enemies; a man to whom it sometimes seemed, in his more irascible and darker moods at any rate, that the only good Gael was a dead one. That phrase, of course, is adapted from a notoriously callous comment made in a part of the world which was just beginning to be opened up in James's day. But in the context of the northward view from Edinburgh Castle, it seems perfectly appropriate. To the men who governed Scotland from this place, in King James's time and later, the Highland Line was not at all unlike America's Indian frontier; and the Gaels, to them, were no more part of civil society than were the Cheyenne or the Sioux.

This makes it all the more curious, I suppose, that the oldest of the many buildings making up the fortress complex which has occupied Edinburgh's castle rock now for the greater part of a millennium was erected on the orders of a monarch who, on his coronation in 1058, can be said without exaggeration to have taken charge of the strongest state which Gaels have ever totally controlled.

Malcolm Canmore's Scotland, for all that the Vikings had deprived it of any jurisdiction over its larger offshore islands, was an altogether more significant kingdom than the country put together by Kenneth MacAlpin some two hundred years earlier. Whole realms had vanished, or been conquered, in the intervening period. Strathclyde was no more; neither was Northumbria. And though King Malcolm's borders with the English were still being vigorously disputed, as they would be for a long time to come, those borders were located more or less where they have ever since remained – on that familiar line between the Solway and the Tweed.

With the Scottish ruling family's successful annexation in the eleventh century of central and southern Scotland, a vast new sphere was opened up – in much the way that Pictland had been opened up before – to penetration by the Gaels. From this time there date the Gaelic placenames which are scattered still across our maps of Ayrshire, Lanarkshire and Lothian. And while it was indubitably the case that Gaels and Gaelic never quite achieved down here – in the vicinity of Edinburgh, in particular – the easy and complete supremacy they had previously established further north, there was no mistaking who was now in charge politically in almost all of mainland Scotland. Malcolm Canmore was a Gaelic-speaking king in a country whose great men were also Gaelic-speakers.

The unity which the Gaels had thus imposed on Alba was all the more impressive in relation to the opposite trends which were then so evident in other parts of Western Europe. The larger part of Ireland had fallen victim to the Vikings, their incursions made much easier by the conspicuous failure of the Irish Gaels to build the solidly constructed sort of state developed by their Scottish counterparts. Elsewhere the great Continental empire established by the Frankish monarch, Charlemagne, was messily disintegrating. And a whole succession of different peoples were attempting to gain mastery in England. In 1066, towards the end of the first decade of Canmore rule in Scotland, the latest of these, led by William of Normandy, would dramatically conquer King Malcolm's southern neighbour.

There was to be no such invasion of Scotland for another two hundred years. But there were to be great changes of another kind; changes which were to undermine, enormously and permanently, the status of things Gaelic in the realm which the Gaels themselves had made; changes which were ultimately to make the Scottish monarchy – still the easily recognisable heir, in Malcolm Canmore's time, of those kings who had been inaugurated in Dalriada – the principal hammer of the Highlanders. And those who have been minded to identify a single villain in this tangled tale have usually looked no further than the woman whose stone chapel still stands here on Edinburgh's dark and dominating castle rock.

Margaret, who was Malcolm Canmore's queen and the mother of three future kings of Scots, is commonly described as English – and in terms which give the impression that she was the virtual puppet of the authorities in London. Matters were never so conspiratorial.

That Margaret was English is quite true. She was descended from the royal house of Wessex, the base from which King Alfred, in the century which also brought the men of Dalriada east to Scone, had begun to shape the first all-English state. But Alfred's heirs had twice been overthrown; initially by the Danes and then by Normandy's Duke William. And Margaret herself had begun her life in distant Hungary. The lady was no simple agent of the kingdom to the south.

That Malcolm's wife was the means of exposing both her husband and her husband's country to external influences of quite a new kind is clear enough, however. She spoke little or no Gaelic. Her sons – Edward, Edgar, Edmund, Ethelred, Alexander and David – were most conspicuously given imported Christian names. And it was at Margaret's instigation that there began to settle in Scotland, initially at Dunfermline, those Benedictine monks who were afterwards to draw the country's church a good deal closer to the European ecclesiastical mainstream – thus helping to complete the process which had begun at Whitby in 664 by eliminating much of what remained of the lingering institutional inheritance of the likes of Colum Cille.

No longer were Scottish monarchs to be buried in Iona. Indeed the island itself, under the terms of a treaty made with the Norwegians by Edgar, King of Scots, in 1098, was formally recognised – as were the rest of the Hebrides – to be a part of Norway. The Scottish kingdom now was visibly cut off from its West Highland origins, looking more to the south and east than in the direction of Ireland, and seeking to model itself increasingly on countries which set not the slightest store on Celtic survivals and traditions of the Dalriadan kind.

The much maligned Queen Margaret gave something of an early impetus to these developments. But she did not reshape Scotland single-handedly. Forces other than those deriving solely from her Wessex background and her Continental upbringing were at work. Not the least of them were those associated with the seemingly unstoppable expansion of the Normans.

England was by no means the last conquest of that most dynamic people. They had spread soon into Wales and into Ireland. They were active, too, in Italy and in the Middle East. It was improbable that Scotland, for all that it was one of the more cohesive of the many realms bordering on the steadily expanding Norman lands, would remain for long immune to their enormous influence. And so things turned out.

In the course of the twelfth century, beginning in the reign of Margaret's younger son, David, and accelerating under the rule of his immediate successors, Malcolm IV and William the Lion, there was a considerable movement into Scotland, from England, of men who, irrespective of their precise territorial origins, had been moulded largely by their prior involvement with the Normans.

One such came north from Shropshire in the 1130s. He was the younger son of a Breton immigrant who had risen high in the service of the English king, Henry I. This latest representative of a clearly ambitious family was to do still better for himself in Scotland. Walter by name, he became chief officer in King

DONALD ANGUS MACLEAN, AMHUINN SUIDHE, ISLE OF HARRIS

David's household. And upon Walter the Steward, as this incoming courtier now became known, his royal master clearly looked with favour. Various lordships were bestowed on Walter by the king who also made it possible for him to marry one Eschina – a lady descended, it was afterwards claimed, from the great men of the long extinct kingdom of Northumbria.

That may have been no more than the genealogical propaganda so habitually put about by up-and-coming individuals seeking to substantiate their claims to power. But whatever doubts there were as to Eschina's ancestors, there were eventually to be none as to the significance of her descendants. Some one and a half centuries after the deaths of Walter and Eschina, the then holder of their family name, Robert Stewart, became himself the king of Scots.

A subsequent Stewart, the one I mentioned as being born here in Edinburgh Castle, would one day unify the Scottish crown with that of England. A later one still – the final representative, in anything but a very complicated sense, of the long line which stemmed from the twelfth-century marriage of Walter

76

and Eschina – was that Prince Charles Edward on whose behalf so many Highlanders were to battle vainly at Culloden.

For all that the last of them has featured now on umpteen million tartan-bordered shortbread tins, the Stewarts never did much good in Gaelic Scotland. The so-called Young Pretender, having failed completely to restore his family's fortunes, served mainly to initiate in the Highlands those transformations which would culminate in happenings of the sort that wiped out Aoineadh Mor. And the Jacobite prince's role in this regard – though a good deal more tragic than the man himself seems ever to have understood – was not wholly inappropriate. After all, the Stewarts – who, from the fifteenth century to the seventeenth, would devote no small amount of ingenuity to eliminating from the Highlands as many as possible of those semi-autonomous institutions which then gave to that region much of its social and cultural distinctiveness – had been identified, from their arrival here in Scotland, with very many of the causes of Scottish Gaeldom's long decline.

It was not simply that Walter the Steward and his like did not speak Gaelic. They did not think or act like Gaels. Their world was one in which the interwoven intricacies of Celtic kinship mattered less than the strictly hierarchical relationships associated with the system of land tenure known as feudalism. And Scotland, as the Norman influence on it grew, was becoming a more feudal country: a land of motte-and-bailey castles built on Norman patterns; a land in which men held their estates increasingly by virtue of Latin charters of the Norman type; a land of sheriffs and of sheriffdoms; a land of traders, merchants and, increasingly, of towns.

Though Fife, for instance, had been for many generations Gaelic-speaking, it is not without significance that a twelfth-century list of the principal men residing in the then recently established burgh of St Andrews deals in the likes of Elfgar, Arnold and William the Cook. These are not Gaelic names. This immediately suggests that power in Scotland's new towns, just like power in much of Scotland's countryside, had begun to slip decisively from the hands of Gaels.

That process did not happen all at once; nor did it happen equally in different places. In Galloway, for example, Gaelic would linger for a long time yet. And as was to occur much more widely in Ireland, there were several Norman families who, on settling in the still more strongly Gaelic Highlands, themselves became completely gaelicised. The Lovat Frasers – one of whom, as a result of his involvement with the Jacobites, would become the last British subject to be beheaded – were among the more significant of these.

Going native in this way was, however, comparatively rare. When Norman immigrant families at last gave up their French, it was not Gaelic which they eventually adopted. Rather, it was the form of speech which had been common in Northumbria, that Anglian dialect whose ancient origins were on the Continent; the language which, having survived the Canmore dynasty's expansion into Lothian, was eventually to become the day-to-day vernacular of Scottish noblemen and kings as well as Lowland commoners. This was the language that a later age would dub Broad Scots. And in the twelfth and thirteenth centuries, in almost all those parts of Scotland outwith the Highland hills, this language gradually began to take the place of Gaelic.

The Scottish monarchy's remoter ancestry had not yet been forgotten. When the seven-year old Alexander III was crowned king of Scots in the summer of 1249, the consequent ceremonials included the reciting – in Gaelic – of the monarch's genealogy; a genealogy, of course, which had its earliest beginnings in Ireland and Dalriada. And when he sought to reverse the English conquest which followed Alexander's most untimely death, Robert Bruce, too, took care to proceed in strict accordance with Dalriadan custom. In 1306, though its sacred coronation stone had been removed now by the invading armies of Edward I, Bruce had himself proclaimed the rightful king of Scots in Kenneth MacAlpin's ancient capital of Scone.

There was no lack of Gaels on Bruce's side when he won his decisive victory at Bannockburn. There were times, indeed, when King Robert seemed to be envisaging something in the nature of a wider Celtic crusade against the now detested English. In 1315, in advance of the military expedition made by his brother Edward to Ireland, Bruce himself addressed to the leaders of the Irish a number of letters in which he stressed the shared origin, the common language and the common customs of both the Irish and the Scots. Though Edward Bruce did not unite Ireland's eternally warring factions for long enough to realise his ambition of ending England's overlordship of that country, he elaborated still further on King Robert's vision of a great anti-English alliance of the Celtic peoples of the British Isles. When Ireland had been liberated, Edward Bruce forecast on one occasion, he would cross to Wales and drive the English from that conquered principality also.

It was not to be, not then and not in the future. Robert Bruce, by far the most outstanding of Scottish monarchs and a man whom Highland tradition still insists was the last of Scotland's kings to speak good Gaelic, was succeeded by men of a very different cast of mind.

King Robert had been raised among the Gaels of Carrick. The likes of James

VI, born here in Edinburgh Castle, the very seat and centre of the Scottish state whose independence Bruce had so successfully preserved, had a very different kind of upbringing. Tutored by men thought then and later to be learned, James would regard all Gaels as savages. His prescription for them was to have them wholly removed from their ancestral lands – whether in the Hebrides or Ireland – in order that the resulting empty spaces might be occupied by those settlers whom James and his lieutenants sought to recruit, for that purpose, in those parts of mainland Britain which they felt to be self-evidently more civilised than the benighted Celtic regions of the west.

This policy failed entirely in the Scottish islands. In Ulster it succeeded. The resulting hatreds and divisions, of which I had seen some hint in Antrim and in Derry, are daily with us still.

CHAPTER FIVE

Although I live in Skye, of all the Hebrides Islay has long been the island I like best. Its people – those whom I know anyway – seem to me to give the place a friendly feel. And it so happens that my visits have practically always coincided with spells of good weather; weather of the kind which produces sunlight strong enough to show the full range of colour contrasts you get around the likes of Loch Indaal. Bright blue waters; bright green fields; clusters of white-painted buildings perched here and there between the two: these are the impressions of Islay which linger in my mind.

This evening, towards the end of August, Islay is not at all like that. The day has been one of the sort which in the west of Ireland they call *tais*, or soft. It is not wet exactly; not even drizzling. But the wind off the Atlantic is so moist as to make the air feel definitely damp. The atmosphere, as a result, has taken on a peculiarly milky quality. The landscape has something of the appearance of slightly faded watercolour. The horizon has no hard edge to it. And when I look out from Bowmore, in the direction of Port Charlotte and Bruichladdich, the rising ground behind these communities seems simply to merge with the steadily lowering clouds.

The road northwards from Bowmore begins by skirting the extensive mudflats at the head of Loch Indaal. Then, just before Bridgend, it plunges suddenly into the heavily wooded policies surrounding Islay House. Here I turn into the shallow valley of the River Sorn, passing a succession of productive-looking farms of the type which, despite the agricultural industry's many recent difficulties, are still common enough hereabouts.

Its underlying Hebridean character is so evident as to make it wrong to say that Islay's farms give its landscape a wholly Lowland look. But they certainly differentiate the place markedly from the predominantly crofting islands further north; as do Islay's several villages which – for all that none of them, not even Bowmore, are very large by mainland standards – are older and more concentrated settlements than those you typically find in the Highland part of Scotland.

A mile or so beyond one such village, Ballygrant, I pause at a junction and take the narrow road to my left. The road soon becomes a track. Once it led to Finlaggan Farm, but the farm has for some time been abandoned. Loose sheets of rusting corrugated iron lie about its overgrown yard. The roofs of its once substantial steadings are collapsing gradually inwards; their rafters projecting from among their thinning slates in much the same way as the ribs of those long dead sheep – which you come across occasionally while walking among the Highland hills – can be seen jutting through the gaps in their tightly stretched and slowly rotting sides.

Agriculture has been recently replaced by forestry in much of this north-eastern corner of Islay, and forestry does not keep people on the land. This is an emptied countryside. Far too many of its cottages and farmhouses have that strangely hollow look you get about a former dwelling when its window-panes and window-frames have gone. Hillsides which once supported sheep and cattle have been given over now to conifers.

Leaving my car at the track's end, I follow the path leading towards Loch Finlaggan. There is more dereliction here. On two small islands, not far from the loch's eastern extremity, are the crumbling remnants of a number of buildings. Standing out darkly against the cloudy western sky and the rough waters of the loch, these ruins, while stark enough, do not seem terribly impressive. They have nothing of the grandeur of Edinburgh Castle. And their surroundings – which consist mostly of gently rounded hills – make this a scenically less spectacular place than, for example, Iona.

'But there was a time when Finlaggan was as important as anywhere in Scotland,' I had been told a little earlier by Islay farmer, Donald Bell. So it was. For Finlaggan, in the fourteenth and fifteenth centuries, was the main centre of the Lordship of the Isles. And it was this semi-independent principality which, for more than a hundred years, went no small way to providing Gaelic-speaking Scots with an organisational focus of the kind which had been lost as a result of the anglicisation of the Scottish monarchy.

Here at Finlaggan, on the larger of these two islands, Eilean Mor, successive Lords of the Isles maintained their most important residence. On the smaller island, Eilean na Comhairle, there met the lordship's governing council. Here, too, as was long afterwards recalled by Hugh MacDonald, a seventeenth-century historian and tradition-bearer from Skye, the Lords of the Isles were formally installed in office – their installation, as described by the Skye *seannachie*, being very reminiscent of the coronation ceremonies once conducted in Dalriada.

A bishop was always present at the inauguration of a Lord of the Isles, MacDonald observed. And the bishop was accompanied, it seemed, by 'seven priests' as well as by 'the chieftains of all the principal families' then occupying the lordship's extensive territories.

At Finlaggan, MacDonald continued, 'there was a square stone, seven or eight feet long, and the tract of a man's foot cut thereon'. Each new Lord of the Isles stood on this carved stone, 'denoting that he should walk in the footsteps of his predecessors'. And it was in this upright position, MacDonald explained, that the lordship's leaders entered into their inheritance.

The Finlaggan stone – which evidently possessed the same sort of spiritual significance as both the Scottish Stone of Destiny and the Irish Stone of Kings on which the O'Neill chieftains of Tyrone were traditionally inaugurated prior to its being smashed to pieces by the English in 1601 – has long since disappeared. It is hard now, on these deserted islands where the summer's growth of waist-high vegetation makes it difficult to discern even the foundations of most of the many buildings which once stood here, to recapture the tremendous sense of occasion which must have surrounded the installing of a Lord of the Isles.

'He was clothed in a white habit to show his innocence and integrity of heart,' said Hugh MacDonald of one of the men whose rule began here in Finlaggan. 'He received a white rod in his hand, intimating that he had the power to govern, not with tyranny and partiality but with discretion and sincerity.' A sword was then handed over, MacDonald continued, in order to signify the means by which the people of the lordship expected their leader 'to protect and defend them from the incursions of their enemies'. These ceremonies being concluded, 'mass was said … the people pouring out their prayers for the success and prosperity of their new-created lord.'

For many years, it seems, these prayers were amply answered. Finlaggan, quite remarkably, was never fortified. Unlike most other magnates of the time – whether in Scotland, England or the Continental countries – the typical Lord of the Isles felt secure enough to occupy a home which, as Lowland chroniclers make clear and as is confirmed by the nature of the Finlaggan ruins, was much more of a mansion than a castle.

The lordship was most certainly not averse to making war. Strung out along the western seaboard, from Skipness in Kintyre to Caisteal Tioram in Moidart, are the still impressive remnants of its many keeps and strongpoints. And on the distinctively sculpted tombstones of the lordship's leading men there can be seen repeated representations of the beautifully constructed and formidably effective galleys on which, more than on anything else, successive Lords of the Isles relied in times of trouble.

But there was more to the lordship than its undoubted military strength. Its castles and its warships protected a society ruled in accordance with customary Gaelic law; a society in which Gaelic culture flourished as it had once done in the wider kingdom of the Scots. The lordship had its dynasties of sculptors, doctors, judges, poets, armourers, metalworkers and musicians; each of them skilled in learning or in crafts which had their origins in ancient Ireland. And of these none was more impressive than the MacMhuirich family, which, generation after generation, produced an unrivalled line of Gaelic bards.

The original MacMhuirich came to Scotland from Ireland in the early thirteenth century, and the fact that some five hundred years later his descendants were still producing Gaelic poetry, was not due simply to their having inherited their literary talents in the way that one inherits blue eyes or red hair. Bardic office of the MacMhuirich type might be transferred from father to son, but successive members of the family were made fit to hold such office – both under the Lords of the Isles and under the Clanranald chieftains to whom they transferred their allegiance following the lordship's ultimate collapse – by a rigorous programme of study and training.

That training, a great deal of which took place in Gaelic Ireland, brought rewards in the shape of the fame and influence which the MacMhuirich family long enjoyed. The territorial possessions granted them by the Lords of the Isles in Kintyre were of high quality, as were the farms they subsequently occupied on the Clanranald lands in Uist. And various members of the MacMhuirich kindred were certainly among the men who gathered here on Eilean Mor at times of public ceremony.

The 'white apparel' worn by the Lord of the Isles on the day of his inauguration was traditionally gifted to a poet, commented Hugh MacDonald. And when, following the satisfactory conclusion of the installation rites, the Finlaggan court and council gave themselves over to feasting and merriment, the lordship's 'bards and musicians' were among those to be most 'liberally' treated.

The ancestry of the Lords of the Isles – and of those subsequent Clan Donald chieftains whose prestige rested, in no small measure, on their kinship with the lordship's ruling family – is habitually traced back to that Somerled whom I mentioned in connection with a half-legendary battle said, by Hugh MacDonald among others, to have been fought in Morvern. That battle, in simpler versions of the tale, involved Gaels on the one side and Norwegians on the other. But it is more than doubtful if, in Somerled's twelfth-century heyday, the parties to any West Highland quarrel could be so conveniently delineated.

Somerled's own name, Sumarlidi, was Norse. He was one of those warrior princes who, for all that they owed a nominal allegiance to Norwegian kings, succeeded – during the fairly lengthy period when all of Scotland's island groups belonged to Norway – in carving out substantial principalities for themselves in the Hebrides.

Somerled was no latterday Viking, however. His own ancestry seems also to have included Gaels, not least among them a member of an Irish aristocratic family who may well have come to Alba to take advantage of the many opportunities arising from Kenneth MacAlpin's expansion of his kingship into Pictland. Those MacDonald genealogies which link Somerled with the Ulster of Colum Cille's time are the product, then, of more than the wishful thinking of bards who were over-anxious to make a connection between Clan Donald's principal originator and the quasi-mythical founders of the Gaelic race. He was certainly descended from other men of power, and not all of these, as one might expect in the racially tangled circumstances of the Norwegian-ruled Hebrides, were of pure Norse extraction.

Whatever his origins, Somerled was clearly able to capitalise on the absence of effective royal authority in the islands. His successors were to do likewise – their freedom of action, in this regard at least, being in no way curbed by the territorial adjustments which followed the Scottish kingdom's victory over King Haakon of Norway in 1263.

The Battle of Largs, together with the subsequent Treaty of Perth, certainly transferred sovereignty in the Hebrides from Norwegian monarchs to the kings of Scots. But the latter found it no easier than the former to exercise real power in the far west. When, in the middle years of the fourteenth century, Somerled's inheritors – those men who ruled so confidently from Finlaggan – took to using, in their Latin charters, the phrase *dominus insularum*, Lord of the Isles, itself merely a translation of their more long-standing Gaelic title of *ri Inse Gall*, they were merely making explicit the political realities of the situation in which they found themselves. Much of the West Highlands, for the greater part of the medieval period, was simply beyond the jurisdiction of Scotland's central government in distant Edinburgh.

This was not a purely Scottish phenomenon. The Welsh principality of Gwynedd and the duchy of Brittany in France are other examples – both of them, incidentally, strongly Celtic in heritage and outlook – of peripheral regions which, at the time when the Lords of the Isles were visibly exerting their autonomy, were also given to conducting themselves as if they were virtually independent of the states of which they were nominally a part. But the fact that other European kings were facing similar threats to their authority did not make it any easier for Scotland's rulers to tolerate the lordship's steadily expanding influence. When, in the early fifteenth century, the then Lord of the Isles, one Donald by name, made to add the territories of the northern Highland earldom of Ross to his already wide dominions, armed conflict between the lordship and the crown became inevitable.

Much was at stake in the ensuing struggle which occurred at a point when Scotland's wider condition was both parlous and confused. The boy king, James I, was a prisoner in England. His regent, the Duke of Albany, the younger son of that Robert Stewart who was the first of his line to sit on the Scottish throne, was both the uncle and the heir of the captive James. As such, he was widely suspected of having far-reaching ambitions of his own. And when, following the death of Alexander Leslie, Earl of Ross, Albany had the earl's female – and thus politically vulnerable – successor declared his own ward, it was equally widely thought that Albany was capitalising on a new opportunity to bolster his own position.

The unfortunate woman at the centre of these manoeuvres was, as it happens, fairly closely related to Albany. But she was also related to the family of Donald, Lord of the Isles, who thus had his own claims on the earldom – claims which he sought finally to substantiate by the exercise of military force.

From his stronghold at Ardtornish in Morvern in the early summer of 1411, Donald marched first on the royal burgh of Inverness. That strategic centre having fallen to him, the Lord of the Isles then turned east, crossed the Spey and advanced, across Moray and Banffshire, into Aberdeenshire. There, at the little township of Harlaw, a mile or so to the north of Inverurie and within twenty miles of Aberdeen, the lordship's troops encounterd their first serious opposition – an army commanded by Albany's principal agent in the north, the Earl of Mar. Battle was quickly joined.

The scene of the fighting is dominated now by the stone tower built here in 1911 by Aberdeen Town Council in order to commemorate the sacrifices made, exactly five centuries before, by those of the city burgesses who were 'chosen', as the burgh register discreetly puts it, to serve with Mar 'against the caterans'. Something of the Aberdeen men's undoubted sense of being engaged in a struggle to defend their society from barbarian attack is preserved in that use of language. A cateran was a freebooter, a robber, a bandit, a thief. And Donald of the Isles, it seemed to some at least of those who stood against him at Harlaw, was properly so described. The Gaels were considered aliens now in Aberdeen; uncouth and uncivilised aliens at that.

The precise extent of Donald's aims at Harlaw will never properly be known. He was himself the grandson, through his mother, of an earlier king of Scots. And he seems to have been in touch, through intermediaries, with the English captors of the youthful James I. Perhaps he aspired to rule all of Scotland – if not in his own right, then possibly with the absent king's tacit connivance, as regent in Albany's stead. That, of course, is speculation. But what is certain is that victory that day for Donald would once more have enhanced the influence and status of Scotland's Gaelic-speaking people.

The anglicisation of the British Isles – which had been underway for several centuries – was, just then, experiencing something in the nature of a marked reverse. In Ireland, as the lordship's ruling family would have been well aware, the recently resurgent Gaels had succeeded in restricting English rule to a narrow band of territory in the vicinity of Dublin. In Wales the great rising of Owain Glyn Dwr had resulted in much of that conquered country being liberated, at least temporarily, by the native Welsh. Might not Scotland's Gaels seek similarly to recapture the role that had previously been theirs at the nation's centre? Might not the Lord of the Isles, already a great power in the land, provide Malcolm Canmore's kingdom with another Gaelic-speaking king?

Great issues were at stake at Harlaw. That is why the battle rivalled Bannockburn and Flodden in its hold on the popular memory; why it gave rise to ballads which, nearly six hundred years after the event, are still sung in Aberdeenshire; why the name of Harlaw is evoked so frequently in Gaelic poetry.

From Harlaw on an afternoon in July, the month which brought the lordship's army to this part of Scotland, I look north across the Urie Burn. The surrounding fields, mostly given over to a quickly ripening crop of barley, are the product of those agricultural improvements which so transformed the Aberdeenshire countryside in the nineteenth century. The landscape of 1411 would have looked much less domesticated. But for all that it is now an extensive modern farm, not the higgledy-piggledy settlement of former times, I can still pick out the buildings of Balquhain where, in the words of one local balladeer, some 'fifty thousand Hielanmen' once mustered.

They were the 'children of Conn', declaimed a MacMhuirich bard of Donald's men, referring – as always on such occasions – to Somerled's claimed descent from one of Gaelic Ireland's most heroic figures; 'children of Conn of the Hundred Battles'; watchful, daring, dexterous, conflict-loving, brave.

'Ferss wis the fecht on ilka syde,' says one of the Aberdeenshire verse accounts of what followed, adding that 'thair wis not sen King Kenneth's day sic strange intestine crewel stryf.' First one side seemed to be prevailing; then the other. And though there was, in the end, no overwhelming victory for either commander, Donald's eastward and southward progress was decisively obstructed; Aberdeen was saved. The lordship's forces withdrew. For the people of Harlaw there remained only 'a weary burying, the like ye never saw'.

In the graveyard of the now ruined church of Kinkell, which stands on rising ground above the River Don just south of Inverurie, is the tombstone of Gilbert de Greenlaw, one of the Aberdeenshire knights killed at Harlaw. Of the more common soldiery of either side there is no trace. Their bones, presumably, are scattered still below those fields of barley, Highlander and Lowlander alike. And it is more than likely that most of the motorists who catch a glimpse of Harlaw's monument from the busy Aberdeen-Huntly road have not the slightest inkling as to what exactly it denotes.

In the kitchen of his farmhouse at Knocklearoch, a little to the south of Ballygrant, I hear from Donald Bell about the efforts now being made in Islay to make people more aware of the island's connections with the lordship. 'When I was a boy I had no idea that Finlaggan was of any importance whatsoever,' Donald says. 'Nobody taught us anything about the place. Nobody encouraged us to take the slightest interest in it.'

That is changing now, he acknowledges. No small part of the change, though Donald Bell is not the sort of man to claim much credit for it, has come about as a result of his chairmanship of the Finlaggan Trust, an organisation dedicated to preserving, investigating and interpreting the surviving ruins on Eilean Mor and Eilean na Comhairle. Funds have been raised. An interpretation centre has been established. The casual visitor can now obtain something of an insight into the workings of the Lordship of the Isles before venturing across the planks which, for the moment anyway, link Eilean Mor with Islay.

On the evening I make the trip here from Bowmore, a fine rain has just begun blowing up the loch on the strengthening breeze. I take shelter in the corner of one of the few walls still high enough to be recognisably a part of a once substantial building. There is no man-made sound to be heard now at Finlaggan. A sheep bleats repetitively on the far side of the water. The waves are surprisingly loud on the shore. The reeds and rushes rattle in the wind.

Here, in 1411, there came the news of Harlaw. At first, perhaps, it did not seem so significant an encounter as it subsequently came to appear; maybe it was considered more a family quarrel than a historic turning point. The Lord of the Isles and the Earl of Mar, after all, were cousins. It is probable that both Mar himself and many – perhaps even most – of his troops were Gaelic-speakers. So the Battle of Harlaw was not a neatly packaged confrontation between the Gaelic and non-Gaelic elements in Scotland.

But the fact that Gaels fought on both sides at Culloden did not make that episode any less of a Highland setback. The same was true of Harlaw. And though, in the post-Nazi era, there is something more than a little bit off-putting about the racial categories he employed, there is no doubting the essential truth of the comment made about the battle by the eminent Victorian historian, Hume Brown. 'Never since that day,' he wrote, 'has Teutonic Scotland been in real danger from the Celtic race.'

The lordship would subsequently win great victories. At Inverlochy in 1431, for instance, an army dispatched against the Lord of the Isles by the now adult James I was so heavily defeated by the Highlanders as to oblige its commander to take ignominiously to the hills in order to save his life. And for all that Harlaw had gone against them, the Lords of the Isles were able eventually to establish themselves in the earldom of Ross – a development which added Skye and Lewis, as well as a huge tract of the northern mainland, to the territories at their disposal. But the acquisition of Ross, just like the success achieved at Inverlochy, served principally to consolidate the lordship's power in the Highlands and Islands. It did little or nothing to expand that power into those regions where the Gaels had once been predominant and where – for a month or two in 1411 – it looked as if they might become predominant again.

It was in this sense that Hume Brown was right. At Harlaw there ended any possibility of reversing the various political and cultural trends which, since the time of Malcolm Canmore, had so conspicuously eroded the status of the Gaels in Scotland. Now successive Lords of the Isles could hope only to defend themselves against the further expansion of royal power. And as Scotland's kings succeeded in enhancing their own position – by eliminating, for example, the threat posed to them by the Earls of Douglas and various other overmighty subjects in the south – the lordship began to look more and more vulnerable.

Its old assertiveness had not yet gone, however. At Ardtornish in the 1460s, a still authoritative, still self-confident Lord of the Isles – seeking, perhaps, to profit from English and Scottish rivalries in much the same way as Somerled and his like had once benefited from their ability to counter Scottish claims with those of Norway – went so far as to conclude a formal agreement with Edward IV of England. This treaty, which was designed to boost the lordship's finances by securing a supply of English gold, was never effectively implemented. But by enabling the government in Edinburgh to brand the Lord of the Isles a traitor to his country, it helped to seal the lordship's fate.

In the 1490s, in the person of James IV, that most energetic of kings, the Stewart monarchs at last destroyed the family of Finlaggan. New expeditions were launched against the lordship. Its lands were declared forfeit. John, Lord of the Isles, was made a royal prisoner. His once proud title, emptied now of its previous significance, was placed in the king's gift.

That title still survives. It is held today by the heir to Britain's throne. Like that same heir's much better known designation, Prince of Wales, this arrangement serves to make a less than subtle historical statement: that neither the English nor the Scottish kingdoms were ever prepared to tolerate anything in the way of Celtic separatism.

Finlaggan's present condition, I suppose, is a further piece of testimony to the same effect. At Edinburgh Castle I had been in no doubt that I was in a place which had once mattered very much. But if you were to judge the lordship's significance on the basis of what is to be seen now at Finlaggan, you would not rate it highly. So it is best, I conclude, on leaving Eilean Mor in the early twilight brought by mist and rain, to think of this place as it must have been and not as it now is.

Here Scotland's Gaelic civilisation flourished confidently for the last time. From this place there was ruled, by Gaels, a wholly Gaelic realm: a recreated, and enormously expanded, Dalriada; a conglomeration of territories which, at their greatest extent, included all the Hebrides, much of mainland Argyll, Morvern, Ardnamurchan, Moidart and the greater part of Ross-shire. Here

Gaels, in a way that they have never subsequently been, were in full charge of their own destinies. No wonder that Finlaggan, in times when the greatness of Clan Donald was long gone, continued to haunt the imagination of so many Scottish Highlanders.

'Alas for those who have lost that company,' runs one MacMhuirich elegy for what it was that had been destroyed. 'Alas for those who parted from that society; for no race is as Clan Donald, a noble race, strong of courage. There was no counting of their bounty; there was no reckoning of their gifts; their nobles knew no bound, no beginning, no end of generosity. In the van of Clan Donald, learning was commanded; and in their rear were service of honour and self-respect. For sorrow and for sadness, I have forsaken wisdom and learning; on their account, I have forsaken all things; there is no joy without Clan Donald.'

The climb to the 750-foot summit of Beinn Tart a'Mhill, towards the southern tip of the Islay peninsula known as the Rhinns, takes me past more ruins. First there is one heap of stones – surrounded still by the greener-than-usual turf always found in the vicinity of former habitation. Then there is another; then a third. Once there was a little township here; one of the many communities whose people were scattered across the world in the course of Islay's nineteenth-century transformation into an island dominated by farms instead of crofts.

Towards the top of the hill, where the people of that long abandoned settlement would once have pastured their cattle, is one of those large boulders commonly deposited in such places by the retreating glaciers of ten thousand or more years ago. It leans slightly in a north-easterly direction. Under the resulting overhang, with its welcome shelter from the prevailing wind, successive generations of sheep have clearly been in the habit of seeking refuge from the rain. As a shower is coming on, I follow their example.

The rain soon stops. But though a few shafts of sunlight are producing quickly moving silvery patches on the otherwise dark surface of the nearby sea, visibility is not nearly as good as it might be. Mist covers the higher reaches of the Paps of Jura. Colonsay is dimly discernible to the north. But of Mull and Iona, both of which are readily to be seen from here on a good day, there is no sign.

From Beinn Tart a'Mhill, looking south, this south-western corner of Islay seems to constitute a perfect triangle. My observation point is at its base. Loch Indaal is to its left, the Atlantic to its right. Just below its tip are the houses of Portnahaven and Port Wemyss. And positioned precisely at its apex is the

Rhinns of Islay lighthouse – marking the spot which thousands upon thousands of Highlanders, taking passage from the Clyde for the United States and Canada, were to remember as having provided them with their last glimpse of Scotland.

A long, low cargo vessel – a container ship, I guess – is this morning pushing north-westwards out of the North Channel and into the open ocean. The sea is white around the vessel's bows. A heavy swell is running from the west and, much nearer to hand, on the offshore reef known as Frenchman's Rocks and on the cliffs to the south of Lossit Bay, the waves are breaking in repeated bursts of spray. To the south-east, across the narrow neck of the Oa, another of Islay's many promontories, I can see, in gaps between the squalls of slanting rain, the Kintyre hills. Southwards, I once or twice think I can glimpse another coast. But this may be just my own imagining; for the sea, in that direction, quickly fades into the mist.

Some hours earlier – at five minutes short of six o'clock, to be exact – the Shipping Forecast on long-wave radio had spoken of a new depression, the latest in a lengthening series, moving towards southern Iceland. In Sea Area Malin, the name given by the meteorologists to the waters around Islay, this would bring gales and heavy rain by afternoon.

But in the Hebrides and the West Highlands the onset of such bad weather is often preceded by a brief spell of slightly clearer air; a pause during which the remnants of the previous storm are swept aside, as it were, to make way for its successor. It is on this that I am now relying to provide me with a better view of what I had principally hoped to see from Beinn Tart a'Mhill.

Inside half an hour, I get my wish. The intermittent rain peters out completely. Though the flat, grey sky warns of another heavier and longer downpour on the way, it is briefly possible to see a reasonable distance. And there, stretching right across the southern horizon, is Ireland.

Looking once again at the hills of Donegal and Antrim, I remember my first visit to this part of Islay. I was in the company of Gilbert Clerk, a Port Charlotte boat builder and a man steeped in the history and tradition of his place. The day was of the sort which, as I remarked some pages back, I tend to associate with Islay – the sky cloudless, the sea marked by only the lightest of breezes. As we came south into the Rhinns, by way of Kilchiaran, scene of an especially notorious clearance in the 1820s, our talk turned naturally to the land over the water.

He had been more than once across there, Gilbert told me. And though he was an old man when I met him, he was keen to go again; for this Islay Gael's feelings for Ireland were not those of the casual visitor. 'We are one people, ourselves and the Irish,' Gilbert said. Since his own perspective on the links between the two sides of the North Channel was one that took account of most things which had happened in both Scotland and Ireland since the time of Colum Cille's voyage to Iona, the political and religious differences which have grown up between the two countries in recent centuries seemed, to Gilbert, no more than the merest of distractions. 'We are one people,' he repeated more than once. 'It is to Ireland, not to England, that we Scots still ought to look.'

More than a century before my conversation with Gilbert Clerk, who is himself now dead, another Islayman, William Livingston, a tailor by profession but a scholar and a bard by disposition, had looked similarly 'over the sea' – as he put in his poem, *Eirinn a'gul*, Ireland weeping – in order to commiserate with his fellow Gaels in what Livingston described as their time of sadness, famine, exile, injustice and grief. As a young man in Islay, Livingston goes on, he had been used to hearing tales of Ireland; ancient stories of a type which portrayed the land behind that intermittently visible coastline as a place of pure enchantment. But now what Livingston calls this fair green country, this home of poetry, music and heroism, had fallen prey to the English foxes. And Ireland, like his native Islay, was being emptied brutally of its Gaelic-speaking people.

A few hundred yards to the south of Bridgend is the commencement of a narrow and twisting hill road which, if I were to follow it south-eastwards, eastwards and then northwards, would take me eventually to Donald Bell's home at Knocklearoch. But today my destination is one more of modern Islay's many former farmhouses – this one turned into a holiday cottage – not much more than half a mile from the road's starting point.

It is the afternoon following my morning trip to Beinn Tart a'Mhill. As the Shipping Forecast had promised, it is raining heavily. The big, hard drops of water rattle loudly on the hood of my anorak as I make my way along a grass-grown gravel track which has the same little-used look as the buildings at its end.

This is Claggan. Here, around 1830, there came a twelve-year old boy whose father was then employed, as he had been for two or three years past, as a gamekeeper on the Islay Estate. The boy's name was John Murdoch, and the man whom he became was to devote no small part of an extraordinarily busy life to reconstructing the long shattered connections between the Scottish Highlands and the nation which William Livingston, very much Murdoch's contemporary, was to lament in his *Eirinn a'gul*.

'The little farm of Claggan,' John Murdoch wrote in his old age, 'had been selected and conferred on my father, I have no doubt, as a favour. The spot was choice in many respects. It was retired and yet not far from people. There was a wood just in front; but the wood being on lower ground, there was a considerable extent of country to be seen over and between the trees. From here I went to school … all the way through the wood and along private paths, hung in the season with woodbine and fragrant also with meadowsweet, thyme and bogmirtle. Wild raspberries were to be found and black bramble berries were abundant. Here also could be found sticks with natural crooks which could be finished off into clubs for the game of shinty.'

Shinty, the Scots variant of the game the Irish know as hurling, is mentioned in the Ulster sagas as one of the several sports of which the young Cu Chulainn was a master. It flourishes still in Skye and many parts of the mainland Highlands. And though shinty has died out now in Islay, it was certainly played here in John Murdoch's day – when, as Murdoch himself was afterwards to recall, the boys of the place were in the habit of staging their matches on the grassy links near the head of Loch Indaal and a little to the west of Islay House.

The then laird of Islay was Walter Frederick Campbell. And one of John Murdoch's shinty-playing friends was the landlord's heir, John Francis. It was, of course, no normal thing in the Highlands and Islands, either then or later, for a gamekeeper's son to have anything very much to do with the children of the 'big house'. But Walter Frederick Campbell was no ordinary landlord. For all that his own surname was, in a sense, commemorative of his clan's triumphant displacement of Islay's earlier MacDonald overlords, Campbell – quite unlike most other members of nineteenth-century Scotland's proprietorial class – was sufficiently attracted to the older ways of doing things to ensure that his son was brought up in a manner not dissimilar to that prevailing in the heyday of the Lordship of the Isles.

'As soon as I was out of the hands of nursemaids,' John Francis Campbell subsequently wrote, 'I was handed over to the care of a piper …. From him I learned a good many useful arts. I learned to be hardy and healthy and I learned Gaelic. I learned to swim and take care of myself, and to talk to everyone who chose to talk to me. My kilted nurse and I were always walking about in foul weather or fair, and every man, woman and child in the place had something to say to us …. I worked with the carpenters; I played … with all the boys about the farm; and so I got to know a good deal about the ways of Highlanders by growing up a Highlander myself.'

As was the case with William Livingston, both John Murdoch and John Francis Campbell heard as lads the stories and the legends which had been current in localities like Islay since Dalriada was first settled by the Gaels; those sagas and tales of Cu Chulainn defeating three times fifty other youths at shinty; of how Conn of the Hundred Battles earned his name and reputation; of how it was that Deirdre came to die.

It was to be John Francis Campbell's great task in later life to begin the systematic collection of that mass of Gaelic lore. By taking down story after story in the words used by those surviving tradition-bearers whom he so assiduously sought out in so many widely separated parts of northern Scotland, he ensured the preservation of much that would otherwise have vanished in the course of the many upheavals precipitated in the Scottish Highlands by those evicting landlords who, for all that their family backgrounds were often similar to Campbell's own, had not one hundredth part of his regard for a language and a culture which they thought, and said, was merely barbarous.

The elder Campbell's eventual bankruptcy meant that John Francis, *Iain Og Ile*, never did become the owner of his father's island estate. But the several books published by this pioneer folklorist, John Murdoch remarked, were 'a more glorious and lasting inheritance' than any piece of landed property. 'They would be remembered,' Murdoch insisted, 'when estates as such are no more and when the world will have forgotten that the Campbells ever held a sod of land in Islay.'

Of course, John Murdoch, whose own travels were to take him in the 1870s and 1880s to practically every corner of the Highlands and Islands, including the Strontian of my Cameron grandfather's boyhood, was not without some prejudice in these matters. Murdoch valued Gaelic with a passion equalled only by the ire aroused in him by landlords. While both of these emotions had their roots in his upbringing here at Claggan, it was his experiences in Ireland, where Murdoch worked as a customs officer in the middle years of the nineteenth century, which gave an overtly political twist to his outlook.

In Dublin, in the 1850s, John Murdoch became deeply involved with a whole generation of Gaelic revivalists, nationalists and radicals of every hue. Adopting the symbolically significant pen name of Finlaggan in order to shield his identity – for this pro-Irish propagandist was, after all, a salaried civil servant – from the British authorities in Dublin Castle, Murdoch wrote article after article on the urgent requirement, in his opinion, for the Irish people to

MAKING HAY BESIDE THE SOUND OF BARRA, ISLE OF SOUTH UIST

'stand shoulder to shoulder' with Scottish Highlanders in a joint campaign for land reform and a measure of self-government.

'The things which we have noted,' Murdoch commented in 1857, at the conclusion of one of his accounts of anti-eviction riots in the Hebrides, 'show that in Scotland the Celt is not going to lie down tamely under the heel of the oppressor; he will be up yet and hand-in-hand with his Irish kinsman will labour for the emancipation of both. May we not look forward to a period not very distant when we shall see the long-separated Gaels of Ireland and Scotland working together for the common good?'

Thanks in no small part to John Murdoch's subsequent efforts, just such an alliance was eventually to be forged. The crofter uprising of the 1880s – which began by propelling Highland issues to the forefront of British politics for the first time since the previous century's Jacobite rebellions and which ended in crofters being granted the security of tenure needed to bring clearance and eviction to an end – was inspired very largely by Irish agitations to which Murdoch, by means of an Inverness newspaper which he founded for that purpose on his retirement from the excise service, insistently drew the attention of his north of Scotland readership.

The Highland Land League – formed at this time to promote the crofting cause – was modelled on a highly successful Irish organisation of the same name. And for all that their Presbyterian clergymen inveighed against the crofting community's growing links with their counterparts in Catholic and nationalist Ireland, an older sense of solidarity prevailed. A Highland Land League candidate, Donald MacFarlane, a man who had himself served previously as Home Rule MP for County Carlow, became the first Catholic to be returned to Parliament from a Scottish constituency in modern times. And when the Irish Land League's founder, Michael Davitt, toured the Highlands and Islands in 1887, with the now elderly John Murdoch at his side, he was fêted everywhere he went.

'Irishmen and Scotchmen,' proclaimed an Argyll newspaper, 'may at last congratulate themselves on having overcome the fierce and brutal prejudices of the past. Mr Michael Davitt, one of the ablest and most persistent of Erin's patriots, has received a welcome in the Highlands which augurs well for the people's cause.'

In the Davitt Museum at Straide in County Mayo – the place from which the Land League hero was evicted with his parents in the course of those famine years which also triggered so many clearances in Scotland – I had seen a memento of that 1887 reception. It took the form of a neatly written 'address' presented to their Irish guest by the hundreds of crofters who attended one of Davitt's open-air meetings at Bonar Bridge in Sutherland. And it occurred to me then, in that neat little building in the west of Ireland, as it occurs to me again this wet September afternoon at Claggan, that John Murdoch and the Highland Land League still await appropriate commemoration in their own country.

CHAPTER SIX

The tide is low this afternoon and, in the bright sunshine which has followed one of the autumn's first frosts, the exposed expanse of seaweed towards the head of Loch Greshornish has taken on a strongly orange tint. To the south, the Cuillin are a crinkle-cut, black backdrop to those nearer and lower hills where the occasional patch of heather gives a splash of sharper colour to a landscape dominated now by the washed-out yellow of the slowly dying deer grass.

Although Skye's tourist season is coming to a close, there are still plenty of coaches in the carpark at Dunvegan Castle. One is German, another Dutch, the remainder from different parts of England. I stop beside one of those. It is owned by a firm whose head office is in Huddersfield. 'Isle of Skye and the West Highlands, Eight Days', proclaims a notice in its windshield.

Our Highland heritage is today big business. History has become a marketable commodity. You want to spend a day examining the Dunvegan archives, trying to find some trace of your Skye ancestors? That will cost you £50. Or maybe you'd prefer simply to stroll through the castle and its grounds? 'That will be £3.30, please,' says the woman at the gate. She does not have an island accent.

Apart from its dungeon – lit by a spooky green bulb and equipped with an electronic mechanism which keeps up an incessantly harsh coughing of the sort which, I suppose, might well have afflicted anyone unfortunate enough to be confined here – the castle interior is disappointingly conventional. Its rooms are in the taste of a nineteenth-century country gentleman. And that is not surprising really, since country gentlemen – of the sort who provided Victorian England with its squires and the British Empire with its officer corps – is exactly what the MacLeods of Dunvegan latterly aspired to be.

But here and there among the settees and the silverware, the regimental colours and the portraits and the photographs of all those successful-looking men and women who, by way of ensuring their acceptability in southern high society, had clearly taken care to put their Gaelic past behind them, there are one or two reminders in Dunvegan Castle of a very different era.

There is, for instance, the heavily decorated drinking cup presented, towards the end of the sixteenth century, to Ruairi Mor, one of the more renowned heads of the Dunvegan family. Like many other of the castle's relics, this one has military associations: Ruairi earned it in battle. But far from fighting for the empire which more than one of his descendants would one day loyally serve, Ruairi Mor MacLeod was on the side of the earliest victims of England's imperial expansion. The cup which the Skye chieftain brought back with him to his stronghold of Dunvegan was awarded him by the O'Neill earls of Tyrone in gratitude for the assistance given them by Ruairi Mor in the course of their ultimately unsuccessful defence of Gaelic Ireland's last semi-independent enclaves against the encroaching armies of England's Queen Elizabeth I.

Here to Dunvegan, at the time of Ruairi Mor, came Mary MacLeod, *Mairi Nighean Alasdair Ruaidh*, the teenage daughter of one of the leading men of Ruairi's clan. In his great house, Mary was to recall in one of the poems she afterwards composed in honour of the Dunvegan chieftain, she had been always joyful. There was dancing then and celebration; fiddle-playing which put her to sleep in the late evening; pipe-playing which woke her in the early morning.

Here, too, came *Niall Mor MacMhuirich*, a member of the bardic family which had earlier served the Lords of the Isles but which was now part of the entourage of those other island chieftains, the Clanranald MacDonalds. Six nights he spent within the walls of Ruairi Mor's Dunvegan, Niall MacMhuirich subsequently recalled; six nights of eating and drinking and music and merriment before the castle's blazing fire; six nights when the sound of the harp mingled with the songs and laughter of the younger members of the household.

There was seemingly no end to the devotion which could be inspired among his people by the likes of Ruairi Mor. 'Their notions of Virtue and Vice are very different from the more civilised parts of Mankind,' reported General George Wade of these Highlanders whom the British government of the 1720s had instructed him to bring to order. 'They think it a most Sublime Virtue to pay

THE CUILLIN FROM SLIGACHAN

a Servile and Abject Obedience to the commands of their Chieftains, altho'
in opposition to their Sovereign and the Laws of the Kingdom, and to
encourage this, their Fidelity, they are treated by their Chiefs with great
Familiarity. They partake with them in their Diversions and shake them by the
Hand whenever they meet them.'

For all that it contained great divergences of wealth and standing, then, this
was no feudal society; no class-riven conglomeration of great territorial magnates on the one hand, and terrorised and poverty-stricken peasants on the
other. This was, as it had been since the heyday of Dalriada, a world founded
– in principle at all times and usually, too, in practice – on ties of blood
relationship; a world in which a seventeenth-century Fraser of Lovat, or
MacShimidh in the Gaelic which the Fraser chieftain's Norman forebears had
adopted centuries earlier, was described as 'so exact in genealogy that he could
give an account of the meanest tenant's origin and parentage, once hearing his
name, whether stranger or native in all his country'.

MacLeod of Dunvegan, Fraser of Lovat, MacDonald of Sleat, MacKenzie of

Seaforth, Cameron of Lochiel, MacNeil of Barra, MacLean of Duart, Stewart of Appin, Grant of Rothiemurchus; very few among them, perhaps, were truly descended from those ancient Irish kings who frequently featured so conspicuously in their various family trees; but all of them – irrespective of the extent to which it suited them to manipulate or even concoct their long and sonorous-sounding pedigrees – lived out their lives in ways which would have been perfectly acceptable in the Ulster of a thousand years before. The immense store set by birth and lineage was part and parcel of this tradition; for in Ruairi Mor's Scottish Highlands, every bit as much as in Colum Cille's Erin, a man's worth depended, first and foremost, on the merits of those he claimed among his ancestors.

But just as the Calvinists who were even then beginning to get a grip on Lowland Scotland reckoned that one of God's elect would necessarily conduct himself in accordance with his peculiarly favoured status, so Ruairi MacLeod and men of his type were expected to make a public display of the virtues inherent in their position. Martial prowess, of the kind which earned the Dunvegan chief the gratitude of the O'Neills, was virtually obligatory. So, too, was lavish hospitality of the kind celebrated in the verse of Niall Mor MacMhuirich and Mairi Nighean Alasdair Ruaidh. Nor is there anything accidental in the extent to which so much of Gaelic literature consists of tribute to the generosity, the bravery, the fine appearance and conviviality of the likes of Ruairi Mor. Bard and chief existed in a kind of symbiosis; the poet depending almost wholly on the great man's patronage; the chieftain equally reliant on the bard for the public recognition which alone could elevate him far above the general run. It was little wonder, in such circumstances, that the MacMhuirichs, in particular, should have acquired eventually the reputation of magicians. Their words could make or break a man more certainly than witchcraft. Their bards, the Roman writer Strabo had written of the Celtic Gauls, were 'held in special honour'; and nearly two millennia on, the same was true of Gaeldom.

Even today, when those kilted and bonneted individuals who like to call themselves clan chiefs are invariably much more at home speaking in the English of their southern public schools than they are in the Gaelic of Ruairi Mor's Dunvegan, there clings still to the literary men and women of the Scottish Highlands – people closer by far to their cultural inheritance than are those folk who now relieve you of your £3.30 at their castle gates – something of that aura which Strabo identified so long ago.

'This had the force of revelation,' wrote the modern Irish poet Seamus

Heaney after hearing his Skye counterpart, Sorley MacLean, *Somhairle Mac Gill-eain*, give a public recitation; 'the mesmeric, heightened tone; the weathered voice coming in close from a far place; the swarm of the vowels; the surrender to the otherness of the poem; above all, the sense of bardic dignity.'

What is true of MacLean, born on a Raasay croft in 1911, was no doubt truer still of those who went before: of Niall Mor MacMhuirich; of Mairi Nighean Alasdair Ruaidh; of all the other members of that self-consciously learned order of poets who so determinedly connected their own times with the distant past. Theirs was no casual, free-and-easy, extemporising sort of art. Rather, it was a strictly governed and rigidly codified means of giving expression to the Gaelic world's long traditional values: to the physical beauty and the highly orna-mented dress on which that world set such store; to the chief as warrior, lover and huntsman; to the open-handedness which always characterises the great man; to the chieftain's sense of honour and dignity; to the magnificence of his possessions; to his ever-important rôle as the protector of his people.

And never had Scottish Highlanders been in so much need of a powerful man's protection as they were in the century which ended with Ruairi Mor ruling in Dunvegan. For while it was the case that much went on in the Highlands and Islands as it had done in the era of the Islay lordship, much had altered also; and often for the worse.

Bards and harpists still made their way, by land and sea, from one great castle to another; the legends of Cu Chulainn continued to be told; the children of the chieftain were fostered still with neighbouring families as they had been when Cu Chulainn's name first featured in Irish story-telling. Among the Gaels, in short, an all-pervading sense of continuity was as strong as it had ever been.

But the Lordship of the Isles had gone; and the monarchy which had willed its destruction had proved incapable, for the moment, of enforcing its own authority in the lordship's place. The time of Ruairi Mor, as a result, was very much a time of troubles; a time still called in Gaelic *Linn nan Creach*, the century of forays; a time when it paid a man to identify himself as explicitly and loyally as possible with a leader strong enough to secure his home and family from the dangers and depredations which threatened on all sides.

The bond between chieftain and clan, of course, was rooted in sentiment, in those feelings of kinship which – whether in Gaul, in Ireland or in Scotland – had always been central to any society made by Celts. So strong were such bonds that they could, for a time at least, survive the chief's own failure to retain his lands. That was why, when James Boswell and Samuel Johnson visited the Campbell property of Iona in the 1770s in the company of Sir Allan MacLean of Duart, the men and women of the island, as Boswell reported, 'ran eagerly' to greet Sir Allan. The Iona people, Boswell went on, 'still consider themselves as the people of MacLean, though the Duke of Argyll has at present possesssion of the ancient estate.'

But those sixteenth and seventeenth-century 'Ilanders' and 'Hylanders' who, as one of their Lowland contemporaries rather despairingly noted, were so ready 'to adventure themselves, their lives and all they have for their masters and chiefes', were motivated by more than pure affection of the kind which James Boswell so strikingly described. In the relationship between a clan and its chief, it seems likely that most pessimistic of political philosophers, Thomas Hobbes – who was just then in England elaborating his singularly gloomy theory of the beginnings of government – would have immediately recognised an actual example of the 'social contract' which, Hobbes thought, had originally been devised to end that 'state of nature' in which man had initially lived.

For just as the earliest peoples, as Hobbes so memorably postulated, had existed in a state of anarchy which ensured that their lives were nasty and brutish and short, and just as early man, so Hobbes theorised at any rate, had tried to bring these miserable conditions to an end by conceding a large part of his previous freedom to a ruler strong enough to guarantee his safety, so Highlanders and Hebrideans in the time of Ruairi Mor had an urgent need to re-establish the security which the Lordship of the Isles had once enforced. It was this security which the chief, however locally and imperfectly, was expected to provide in return for the quite unstinting loyalty of his clan.

Some three or four miles east of Dunvegan, on the main road to Portree, is Fairy Bridge. Here, in a natural amphitheatre much favoured by local crofters as a rallying place in the Land League years of the 1880s, a MacLeod chieftain – according to Gaelic legend – once took his tearful farewell of the elfwoman with whom he had spent twenty years in the netherworld. But before departing for ever from her mortal lover, the fairy handed over a gift to the MacLeod warrior – a banner which, she said, he was to raise if ever his clan was in danger. This was *a' bhratach shith*, the fairy flag, and it is to be seen still in Dunvegan Castle. Of Middle Eastern origin, and made from a material woven at about the time of Colum Cille's coming to Iona, the banner may have been brought to Skye by the MacLeod's Viking predecessors, some of whom are known to have voyaged far into the Mediterranean. But whatever its precise origins, the fairy flag was thought to be a talisman of quite extraordinary power, and there were to be occasions, in the dreadfully unsettled decades following the lordship's overthrow, when the MacLeods would have much need of it.

From Fairy Bridge a narrow road takes you north into Waternish. The sea is to your left and far below you. The coast is rocky here and the crofting townships of Lusta, Hallin and Hallistra, to which the road gives access, are strung out along the line of the 250-foot contour, the few trees in their gardens bent and twisted by the prevailing south-westerly wind which, the day following my visit to Dunvegan, is driving squalls of rain in from the Minch. The Outer Isles of Harris and the Uists cannot be seen this afternoon. Even the dark cliffs of Dunvegan Head, some five or six miles distant, are now and then obscured by an especially heavy shower.

It was just such a shower, tradition has it, which a party of fishermen – shooting their nets in these still rich waters – thought responsible for a darkening of the starry sky to the west of them one night some four hundred years ago. But the sounds coming to them on the breeze, the netsmen quickly realised, were not those of approaching rain and wind. They were the sounds of creaking ropes and straining masts; the noises made by vessels under sail. The galleys of the Clanranald MacDonalds were on the Minch. That was not likely to augur well for Skye.

The fishermen now cut their nets adrift and headed shorewards with all the speed they could muster. Behind them, and closing swiftly on their little coble, was one of Clanranald's fastest birlinns, its crew eagerly fitting arrows to their bows. Landing somewhere below the modern crofting settlement of Galtrigill, a mile or so to the north of Borreraig, home for several centuries to MacLeod of Dunvegan's MacCrimmon pipers, the fishing party ran for the shelter of some rocks. But arrows now were flashing all around them and a detachment of Clanranald's men were in pursuit. The fishermen died just above the shore – except, the story goes, for their skipper, a man known locally as Big Finlay of the White Plaid on account of his great size and his predilection for clothes that were a little bit out of the ordinary.

Fionnlaidh Mor managed to outdistance every one of the MacDonalds. South he ran through Borreraig and Husabost, Totaig, Colbost and Skinidin, until he came at last to Uiginish, a good six or seven miles from his starting point. Dunvegan Castle is separated from Uiginish by a stretch of water nearly half a mile across. But Big Finlay's voice was as powerful as the man's physique. Soon MacLeod himself had been roused by his shouting and preparations for battle were being quickly put in hand.

The MacDonald raiders, meanwhile, had landed in the early morning, and under cover of a thick mist, at Ardmore Bay. On the afternoon of my visit to Waternish, looking down from the vantage point provided by the modern road and seeing the way in which the bay is sheltered so completely from the gathering storm in the Minch by the southward-jutting promontory to which it owes its name, it is easy to understand its attractions as an anchorage.

The land is good and green here. Inevitably, therefore, the place had been selected for settlement by the Columban monks of nearly a thousand years before. More than one religious building no doubt occupied the site in the intervening period. But the ruins of the church which stood here at the time of the Clanranald landing can still be seen on the steeply rising ground above the beach.

The Uistmen came ashore at Ardmore on a Sunday. The people of the place were all at worship. There was nobody about to observe the raiders stealing quietly up on the church in the fog still swirling off the sea. Nor was there anyone to interfere with their hurried barring of the door, their hastily setting fire to the roof of thick straw thatch.

How many Waternish folk were killed here that day no one now can say. But of the entire congregation, it is traditionally insisted, only one escaped both the flames and the weapons of the waiting MacDonalds. She was a young woman who managed to squeeze through a window which, if it was of a similar pattern to the one which can still be seen in the building's surviving eastern gable, was no more than six inches wide. This girl, it is said, belonged to Unish, a now deserted hamlet just south of Waternish Point. And even she was badly hurt that terrible Sunday morning, dying of her wounds at a nearby well which was long to bear her name.

To Ardmore Bay there now came hastening the chief of Dunvegan and his men. With them they carried *a' bhratach shith* as well as their bows and swords and axes. And before the MacDonalds could take ship again for Uist, the MacLeods were on them, killing practically every one of Clanranald's people and burying them under a convenient turf dyke, or wall, which the victorious MacLeods toppled on to the Uistmen's cut and mangled corpses.

For all that this Battle of the Spoiling of the Dyke, as the Ardmore episode is remembered in MacLeod tradition, was retrospectively to take on something of that stirring quality which still pervades the pibroch composed in its commemoration, it is doubtful if, to most of those who were directly affected by such atrocities, the horrific suffering associated with clan warfare was made any less unbearable by the art which it inspired. The Dunvegan family's

MacCrimmon pipers, just like Clanranald's MacMhuirich bards, were unrivalled masters of their trade. But even they were hard put to turn into the stuff of heroism some of what was done by the men to whom they owed their privileged position.

The MacLeods themselves had earlier massacred the greater part of the MacDonald population of Eigg. The Glengarry MacDonalds, in a virtual re-enactment of what occurred at Ardmore, were to incinerate a congregation worshipping in an Easter Ross church. Both Clanranald and MacNeil of Barra were to engage, from time to time, in piracy. And more than one struggle for local supremacy was to take on the character of all-out conflict.

At Carinish in North Uist you might still be shown, if you ask locally, the ditch which is said to have run red with blood when the MacLeods and the MacDonalds battled here. And far to the south, on the wide expanse of flat land at the head of Loch Gruinart in Islay, where the Royal Society for the Protection of Birds has now established a nature reserve, other MacDonalds fought so savagely with the MacLeans of Duart that, when the day was done, some three hundred men lay dead.

Scottish Highlanders had long been famed for their skill in war. They had fought with Bruce and other kings of their own country. They had seen much service, too, in Ireland where the *gall-oglaich*, or gallowglasses, the name given to a whole class of professional soldiers from the Gaelic-speaking parts of Scotland, were long familiar figures.

The gallowglass, in his earliest thirteenth or fourteenth-century incarnation, was a heavily armed infantryman, dressed in a conical iron helmet and a chain-mail coat, and wielding – usually to deadly effect – a two-handed battle-axe of a design which undoubtedly owed its inspiration to the very similar weapon first brought to the Hebrides by the Viking raiders of several centuries before.

By the more fastidious standards of a later age, the gallowglass was a mercenary. But for all that he may have sold his services for cash, the typical gallowglass – in his own eyes and, indeed, in those of most of his contemporaries – was no simple, hired-out footslogger. Rather the reverse; for with his expensive equipment, carried for him by his personal servant, and his readily apparent air of being a person of some military consequence, the gallowglass, with not a little justice, habitually thought himself a cut above the herd.

Some at least of the Skyemen who accompanied Ruairi Mor MacLeod to Connaught in the 1590s were in the gallowglass tradition: high-born individuals who – though they would have thought it quite beneath their dignity to engage in agriculture or other menial activity of that kind – were quite prepared to sell themselves as soldiers in other people's wars.

The imposition of effective English rule in Ireland was to close off the traditional external market for the martial energies of Scottish Highlanders. But other outlets were quickly made available. The forces of two of seventeenth-century Europe's more aggressive monarchs, Gustavus Adolphus of Sweden and Louis XIV of France, were to have their stiffening of Gaels. And nearer home, of course, men of the sort who had in earlier times been known as *gall-oglaich* were, in their later guise of *daoine-uaisle* (the designation given to the gentry of the seventeenth or eighteenth-century Highland clan), to provide the backbone of those armies raised by the likes of the Marquis of Montrose and Prince Charles Edward Stuart.

But even Montrose and the Jacobites were engaged in causes which were not primarily Highland. And it was to be a major element in Gaeldom's looming tragedy that, with the passing of the Lordship of the Isles, there was no single institution with the capacity to organise the substantial military manpower of the Scottish Highlands and apply that manpower in ways which were explicitly designed to serve a Highland purpose.

On the Heights of Abraham with Wolfe, at Corunna with John Moore, at Waterloo with Wellington, and on another hundred British Empire battlefields, Highlanders would one day earn a worldwide reputation as virtually unbeatable fighting troops. It was their desperate misfortune that, for several generations prior to their being mobilised beneath the banner of the Union Jack, the men of the Scottish Highlands warred mostly with each other.

Such was the enduring magic of the lordship's name and reputation that it was inevitable that some attempt would be made to restore the family of Finlaggan to their former greatness. And when, in the 1540s, a force of 4,000 men and 180 galleys was raised by Donald Dubh, grandson of the last Lord of the Isles, with a view to regaining his ancestral title, there seemed, for a moment, some prospect that the earlier forfeiture might yet be set aside.

For all that the people of the Hebrides and the West Highlands promptly identified themselves with Donald's cause, however, their rallying to him did them no more good than their subsequent, and equally enthusiastic, adherence to Prince Charles Edward Stuart. Donald died before his military preparations could be properly put to the test. All that disguised the extent to which his now leaderless followers were at the mercy of their enemies was the fact that the sixteenth-century Scottish government lacked the ability of its eighteenth-century British successor to impose its will conclusively upon the Scottish Highlands.

Having destroyed the Lordship of the Isles, but being without the capacity to fill the political vacuum left by its demise, the royal authorities in Edinburgh were forced to rule largely by proxy in the north and west. Wishing to tame the more unruly and insubordinate clans, they turned – in anticipation of a strategy that was also to be adopted, for very similar reasons, in officialdom's dealings with the Indian tribes which occasionally menaced colonial Britain's North American frontiers – to those other clans on whom they thought they could depend. Thus the MacKenzies of Seaforth were encouraged to displace the MacLeods of Lewis. And the Campbells of Inveraray became the willing means by which the various kindreds of the lordship's Argyll heartland were gradually deprived of their former standing.

In their centuries-long effort to wrest from Clan Donald the poetic – but politically portentous – title of *Ceannas nan Gaidheal*, the headship of the Gael, the Campbells did not seek to make themselves an independent power. That had been the tactic of the MacDonald Lords of the Isles. But it had not worked; not in the long run, anyway. And the Campbells – whether coincidentally or not – almost invariably followed a diametrically opposite course. They made themselves the indispensable Highland allies of central government. They took care to ensure that their ceaseless expansion had the sanction of the Edinburgh political establishment. They took equal care to have their conquests backed by legal documentation as well as by their swords.

This was a strategy on which Jacobite poets such as Alasdair MacMhaighstir Alasdair were invariably to pour much scorn. But it had been bringing valuable dividends to Inveraray ever since one of the earliest Campbells had allied himself with Robert Bruce in the course of the latter's ultimately successful campaign against the MacDougalls who were then the principal family in Argyll. In the fifteenth, sixteenth, seventeenth and eighteenth centuries it was to make *MacCailein Mor*, the Campbell chieftain, first an earl, then a duke. It was also to make him one of the foremost landed magnates in the British Isles.

Kintyre, Islay, Mull, Iona, Morvern and Tiree – all of which, in the heyday of the lordship, had been held either by the MacDonalds or by their MacLean subordinates – now passed into the hands of MacCailein Mor and his kin. That alone would have been sufficient to make the name of Campbell highly suspect among those clans which were – or felt themselves to be – threatened by Mac-Cailein Mor's ambitions. But it was in the nature of the sort of society then prevailing in the Highlands and Islands for some clans to expand at the expense of others. And the sheer intensity of the animosity engendered so widely by the Campbells is not to be explained solely in terms of their territorial aggrandisement.

What made Campbell expansionism so especially hard to bear was the extent to which it came to be considered – quite correctly – as the product of an alignment between one part of Gaeldom, Clan Campbell itself, and those essentially extraneous forces, represented first by Scottish and then by British governments, which were increasingly determined to subvert or destroy not just this clan or that clan but the entire social and cultural order, of which clans were simply the most visible manifestation.

Because the Scottish kingdom had been created by Gaels and, for several centuries, had been ruled by Gaels, there were to begin with few of those divergences between Highlands and Lowlands which, more recently, we have come to consider virtually axiomatic. Geography and climate, of course, imposed their own regional variations. But in the time of Malcolm Canmore, or even in the time of Robert Bruce, there was little or no sense – in any quarter – of Highlanders being in some way a people apart.

Those changes which had begun in southern Scotland in the time of Queen Margaret and Walter the Steward, however, were soon weakening this older solidarity. In the chronicle compiled in the 1380s by the Aberdeenshire priest, John of Fordun, there thus becomes apparent a wholly novel distinction between Lowlanders, on the one hand, and Highlanders, on the other. That distinction is made in terms which were to become all too familiar in the years which followed.

'The manners and customs of the Scots,' wrote Fordun, 'vary with the diversity of their speech. For two languages are spoken amongst them, the Scottish and the Teutonic; the latter of which is the language of those who occupy the seaboard and the plains, while the race of Scottish speech inhabits the highlands and the outlying islands. The people of the coast are of domestic and civilised habits, trusty, patient and urbane, decent in their attire, affable and peaceful, devout in Divine worship, yet always ready to resist a wrong at the hands of their enemies. The highlanders and people of the islands, however, are a savage and untamed race, rude and independent, given to rapine, ease-loving, clever and quick to learn, comely in person but unsightly in dress; hostile to the English people and language and, owing to this diversity of speech, even to their own nation. They are also exceedingly cruel.'

BEINN TIANABHAIG FROM THE CREAG MHOR, ISLE OF SKYE

Fordun, interestingly enough, made no mention of the clan, which later commentators were often to regard as the defining feature of the Highland scene. Nor was this any mere oversight on the chronicler's part. Despite his clear commitment to the emerging Lowland world with which he so explicitly identified himself, it would simply not have occurred to Fordun to differentiate that world from its Highland counterpart in terms of its social organisation.

For all that feudalism had made more progress to the south and east of the Highland Line than it ever did to the north and to the west of that divide, the Lowlands, too, retained something of the Celtic character imparted to them by the Gaels. Continental visitors to medieval Scotland were clearly struck by the Scottish population's evident lack of that submissiveness which they took for granted in their own countries. While the relationship of a Lothian or Aberdeenshire tenant to his lord was clearly far from identical to that prevailing between Ruairi Mor MacLeod and his people, it nevertheless had much more in common with Highland clanship than it had with the grovelling subservience demanded of their peasantries by French or English noblemen.

The Scottish Lowlands, in the Middle Ages, were not without their conflicts. But they experienced no peasant revolts of the kind which were happening elsewhere. As was equally true of the Highlands and Islands, Lowland quarrels tended to be associated much more with cleavages between rival families or kindreds than with animosities between different social classes. This was no longer the case, to be sure, by the eighteenth century. Then the nature of the connection between one Lowlander and another was increasingly likely to have more to do with cash than kinship. It was in these transformed circumstances that those Jacobite regiments raised by the likes of Cameron of Lochiel or Stewart of Appin were inclined to take on, in the eyes of the frightened citizenry of the Central Belt, something of the character of a half-legendary monster come suddenly to life.

Earlier Cameron or Stewart chiefs, however, were a lot less readily distinguishable from their Lowland counterparts. The sixteenth-century Aberdeen historian, John Major, was writing of the connection between Lowland farmers and their locally resident magnates when he commented: 'They keep a horse and weapons of war and are ready to take part in his quarrel, be it just or unjust ... and with him, if need be, to fight to the death.' But Major could just as easily have been describing the situation then to be found in places like Skye or Lochaber. He consequently saw nothing very remarkable in clans.

Though he was every bit as ready as Fordun to differentiate Scotland's *domestica gens* from its *ferina gens*, its civilised folk from its savages, Major – in attemping to explain what it was that separated the one from the other – tended, like his predecessor, to focus on the fact that the latter group, the Highlanders and Islanders, spoke their own distinctive language. This language, of course, was Gaelic. At one time it had been described by the Latin-using John of Fordun and other early chroniclers as *lingua Scotica*, the speech of the Scots, whose native tongue it had been ever since the Scoti, or the Gaels, had begun to settle in Dalriada. But now the term 'Scottis', or Scots, began instead to be applied to the tongue previously known as 'Inglis', or English – the formerly Northumbrian language which, some time before John Major set his pen to parchment, had become the everyday vernacular of almost all of Lowland Scotland.

This was the language in which the fourteenth-century churchman, John Barbour, would compose his epic poem, *The Brus*, in praise of Scotland's liberator king; it was the language in which there were preached the sermons which ushered in the Protestant Reformation; the language in which Robert Burns would one day set down his verse. And on its being applied more and more to national purposes, on its becoming the day-to-day speech of king and commoner, of the church and the law-courts, the ale-house and the market-place, it was inevitable that Scots, among Lowlanders at least, should have become increasingly a badge of Scottishness – to the extent that the Gaelic of the Highlands and Islands, as began to occur in John Major's time, came to be described as 'Irish' or 'Erse'.

King James IV, for all that he devoted so much of the earlier part of his reign to the overthrow of the Lordship of the Isles, was reported by one foreign observer to have learned 'the language of the savages who live in some parts of Scotland'. But this was now exceptional. By most Lowlanders, from the monarch in Edinburgh Castle to the lowliest occupant of the meanest farm cottage, Gaelic was commonly regarded as uncouth, backward, barbaric, outlandish, even foreign.

The Highlander was now, as he was to remain for generations, something of a figure of fun. As early as the fifteenth century, the Elgin priest, Richard Holland, was incorporating the common Gaelic greeting, *Beannachd Dhe*, God's blessing, into a scathing satire on 'a bard out of Ireland with Bannachadee'. To Holland's Lowland ear the unfortunate bard's poetry is simply gibberish. 'Glunton guk dynynd dach hal mischy doch,' he has his victim proclaim.

Something of the same disparagement is evident in the sixteenth-century Scots poet who, having explained how God formed the first Highlander from a lump of horse manure, has this exchange take place between the Gael and his creator:

'Quoth God to the Helandman – Quhair wilt thou now?
I will doun to the Lowland, Lord, and thair steill a kow.'

But for all their elevation of their own 'Inglis' as 'fairer' and 'mair parfyte' than the Gaelic 'blabber' of those Highlanders of whom they thus made a mockery, the Lowland authors of such lines, while certainly contemptuous of the Gaels, remained a little apprehensive of them, too. Such fear was well founded, for raids and forays of the type which resulted in so much misery in places like Eigg and Waternish could not forever be confined to those localities which lay beyond the Highland Line.

Although Lowlanders – in a complete overturning of historical realities – were sometimes to insult Highlanders and Hebrideans by implying that they were not Scottish, that particular affront was not reciprocated. The Gaels, being more aware than their tormentors of how the Scottish kingdom was originally put together, always regarded the Lowlander as *Albannach*, Scottish. And that sense of underlying unity, on the Highland side at least, was strong enough to survive persecution, massacre, military repression and eviction. To none of these did Gaels respond by endeavouring to develop a sense of national identity over and above that which they felt themselves to share with the many Lowlanders – from James VI to Patrick Sellar – who devoted so much effort to their effective elimination.

But if the Lowlander was indubitably a Scot, he was, from the Highland point of view, a decidedly second-rate sort of Scot. The Gaels, reported Edmund Burt, an Englishman who spent a good deal of time in Strontian and other parts of the Highlands and Islands in the 1720s, 'have an adherence to one another as Highlanders, in opposition to the people of the Low Country whom they despise as inferior to them in courage, and believe they have a right to plunder them whenever it is in their power. This last arises from a tradition that the Lowlands, in old times, were the possession of their ancestors.'

The 'tradition' which Burt thus came across in the eighteenth-century Highlands was nothing more or less than a lingering recollection of the key rôle played by the likes of Kenneth MacAlpin and Malcolm Canmore in the formation of the Scottish state. And if Burt and others who made similar comments are to be believed, this feeling of having somehow been cheated of their Lowland inheritance served to buttress Gaels in their conviction that – irrespective of what might or might not have been entered in the Edinburgh law books – there was nothing very fundamentally wrong in a Highlander helping himself to the cattle and other movable goods belonging to those Lowlanders unfortunate enough to live in districts handily adjacent to the Highland Line.

Twentieth-century Highlands and Islands poachers, for all that they may be treated as criminals by the courts, are similarly fortified by an unalterable belief that laws reserving the hunting of deer or the catching of salmon to estate proprietors can be categorically dismissed as the work of pro-landlord legislators with a vested interest in giving a spurious legal sanctification to the gargantuan theft perpetrated by those noblemen who long ago took it upon themselves to appropriate natural resources which had previously been treated as community assets. It is in this sense that the man who takes a salmon from a landowner's river – as I have done myself on occasion – stands, to some small extent at least, in the shoes of those of his ancestors who once came at night to carry off the Lowland farmer's livestock.

Such practices seem to have begun – and the overlap goes some way to explain the chronicler's all too evident dislike of Gaels – at about the time that John of Fordun was penning his celebrated denunciation of Highlanders. In 1391, for example, a Pluscarden monk describes 'the whole country' as 'troubled' by 'the savage Scots'. Angus, in particular, had had 'no peace because of their marauding'. And when the 'Heylandmen' once again descended on the county in the following year they were said to have come in such strength as to have been able readily to hold their own against a force of armoured knights led by Sir David Lindsay of Glenesk.

Throughout the following century 'the wyld and wykkyd Helandmen' turned up repeatedly in Moray, Aberdeenshire, Angus and Stirlingshire. But for all that the Scots Parliament and Privy Council directed Act after Act against those whom their members called caterans – a word which was derived from the Gaelic *ceathairne*, signifying a lightly armed warrior, but by which the lawmakers meant merely thieves and bandits – there was little that could be done to stop rustling and raiding as long as large tracts of the Highlands and Islands remained beyond the jurisdiction of any very effective law and order.

It was in this respect, moreover, that the Highland policy of successive Edinburgh administrations tended to make things worse rather than better. Those institutions which had earlier helped to keep in check the more unruly impulses of Highlanders – most notably the Lordship of the Isles – were themselves subverted by the central government precisely because the authority they exerted was so great as to be intolerable to monarchs who felt increasingly that all power should be in their own hands. But because the Scottish monarchy's desire for political influence tended to exceed its capacity to exercise such influence over its entire territory, the net effect was to produce in much of the Highlands and Islands conditions of the sort which led to feuds and massacres of the Waternish type as well as to sorties of the kind which blighted Angus.

So it came about that the Highlands and Islands became irredeemably associated, in the mind of Edinburgh legislators, with freebooting and disorder. Nor did Lowland hostility to Gaels lessen with time. As the sixteenth century turned into the seventeenth, as conditions in the Lowlands became more settled, as towns grew, as trade expanded, as Lowlanders fervently embraced a fundamentalist Protestantism of the sort which was not to catch on in the Highlands for another two hundred years, so the differences between Lowlander and Highlander became steadily more marked. All of this – when added to the constant irritant of cattle raiding and the intermittent threat of organised Highland rebellion – constituted a standing challenge to those Lowlanders who believed, quite understandably from their perspective, that the Highland way of life was both an affront to Lowland values and an obstacle in the way of creating a more united, more modern and more powerful Scottish state. Thus the Gaels, whose country – in a very real way – Scotland was, became pariahs in the nation they had made.

Highlanders in general, and West Highlanders and Hebrideans in particular, declared the Scottish Privy Council in 1600, were wholly 'void of the knawledge and feir of God'. They delighted in 'blude, murthour and all kynd of barbarous and beastlie cruelteis'. Their conduct was a permanent 'reproche' to Scotland.

King James VI and his closer advisers were in full agreement. Andrew Knox, whom James made Bishop of the Isles, described his flock as a 'falss generation', a 'pestiferous' people, a race given over entirely to 'barbaritie and wiketnes'.

Gaelic, thought King James, should be eradicated. It was essential that the 'Inglishe toung be universallie plantit and the Irishe language, whilk is one of the cheif and principall causis of the continewance of barbaritie and incivilitie amongis the inhabitantis of the Ilis and the Heylandis, be abolisheit and removit.'

Only the incorrigible idleness and backwardness of their people, the king believed, were preventing the Highlands and Islands from flourishing economically. The Western Isles, he continued, were 'inrychit with ane incredibill fertilitie of cornis and store of fischeings'. All this, unfortunately, was being set at nought by the 'barbareitie and inhumanitie' of the Hebrideans. What was required, therefore, was that the islands be 'planted' with Lowland colonists; honest folk who would 'advance and set fordwart the glorie of God, the honour of their native countrey and His Majesteis service.'

Thus began the attempt to settle the so-called Fife Adventurers in Lewis where the rule of the island's MacLeod chieftains had been terminated by legal procedings not dissimilar to those previously employed in the case of the Finlaggan MacDonalds. But for all that Lewis was now lost forever to the MacLeods, it was not about to become the permanent possession of the Fife lairds and merchants who were intended to be the means of imposing Lowland schools, Lowland churches, Lowland manners and the Lowland language on its people.

Lewis, despite the king's hopes to the contrary, did not offer rich lands of the sort that were to be got, for instance, in Ulster – where an identical 'plantation' policy was to have the enthusiastic backing of King James following his elevation to the English throne in 1603. Island Gaels, as a result, did not have to confront overwhelming odds of the kind which faced their Irish counterparts. Lewis was simply not sufficiently attractive to ensure that colonists would come in large enough numbers, and with the necessary resources, to ensure the settlement's success.

The Fife Adventurers failed to establish themselves. Nothing came of another scheme by King James to equip Islay with 'burrow touns, with civile people, religioun and traffique of merchandice'. All that could be done, in the short run, was to replace Lewis's MacLeod chieftains with the rather less independent-minded MacKenzies of Seaforth and to engineer circumstances designed to ensure that Islay passed firmly – as it did, in fact, in 1612 – into the clutches of the still more amenable Campbells.

But the Scottish government, it was increasingly borne in upon even those chiefs – like Ruairi Mor MacLeod – whose position remained comparatively secure, was now becoming much more active in the Highlands and Islands than it had ever been before. King James might have taken himself off to London, but as the first man to rule all of the British Isles, and as a Scot who, in the manner of so many of his countrymen both before and since, was extraordinarily anxious to be held in high regard by English people, James was determined to demonstrate that his native Scotland was not a place prepared to tolerate socially deviant behaviour of the kind which remained so distressingly prevalent among the Gaels.

In 1608 the Edinburgh administration accordingly mounted a major expedition to the Hebrides. A number of island chiefs were taken prisoner and removed to various Lowland jails and dungeons from which they were released only on giving certain assurances to the government. Of these the most important was that they would attend a council to be called on Iona by the now absent king's agent, Andrew Knox – that Bishop of the Isles whose low opinion of his spiritual charges has already been made clear.

Ruairi Mor had evaded capture the summer before, but he clearly felt obliged to answer Bishop Knox's summons to Iona in August 1609. There he put his name, alongside that of several more of the leading men of the islands, to a series of nine 'statutes'. These obliged the signatories to assist with the spread of the Reformed Church, to ban the carrying of arms, to send their heirs south for a Lowland education, to establish schools and generally to reduce the size of their own households – not least by removing from these households those bards and musicians whom men like Knox had concluded, quite correctly, to be the main repositories and exponents of traditional Gaelic values.

It may be that men of Ruairi Mor's stamp thought the Statutes of Iona to be of no great consequence. If so, they were wrong. No such measures, of course, were likely by themselves to result in the immediate transformation of the Highlands and Islands. But the forcible seizure of so many powerful individuals – like the loss of Islay to the Campbells, the loss of Lewis to the MacKenzies and the loss, for that matter, of so much of Gaelic Ulster to that province's Lowland and English settlers – showed that the likes of Ruairi Mor were no longer masters of their fate. At Iona in the summer of 1609 – no doubt because they felt themselves to have no very plausible alternative short of an all-out uprising of the kind which, as Ruari Mor knew very well, had failed so totally in Ireland – they compromised decisively with central authority.

Many Highlands and Islands chieftains would subsequently wriggle out of the commitments given to Bishop Knox. Not a few would more than once take up arms against both Scottish and British governments. But the road on which Ruairi Mor and his fellows set foot that August day on Colum Cille's island would, one way or another, be followed to its very bitter end. Gaelic Scotland's own leaders, its clan chiefs, had signalled their willingness, in principle, to act in ways which they must have known to be destructive of the society of which their families had for so long been a part.

The pact thus made between the Edinburgh government and the Gaelic aristocracy of the Scottish Highlands would preserve most of the latter from the death and exile suffered by so many of their Irish counterparts. That is why there is still a MacLeod at Dunvegan. But such survival had its price. The smaller part of that price was the extent – readily evident from the nature of the more modern mementoes scattered through Dunvegan Castle – to which the descendants of Ruairi Mor were obliged to reject their own background; to integrate, and ingratiate, themselves with the Lowland and English establishment. The greater cost was the one borne by the descendants of those of Ruairi Mor's folk whose place had always been outside the castle walls.

South of Dunvegan, scattered around a succession of tidal creeks and inlets at the head of Loch Bracadale, are the townships of Roag, Vatten, Harlosh and Balmore. Here, one night in 1739, there landed a band of men whose task it was to earn good money for a MacLeod chieftain, first by kidnapping and abducting that chieftain's own tenants, and then by shipping their captives as indentured labourers – this being a status not too far removed from slavery – to the British colonies in North America.

By such means did the MacLeods of Dunvegan demonstrate that they had put aside the bonds of kinship; that they had adopted, once and for all, the more commercial, more hard-headed, more self-interested outlook which James VI and Bishop Knox had urged upon them. And as you head still further south towards Sligachan, through Bracadale and Glen Drynoch, seeing here and there the remnants of the settlements which nineteenth-century MacLeods of Dunvegan emptied of their people to make way for those sheep farmers who paid bigger rents than any crofter ever could, you can try – on looking at the desolation which has taken the place of community – to take such comfort as you can from the reflection that, where there was once considered to be nothing but barbarity, there is now civilisation.

CHAPTER SEVEN

I have come to Lochaber on an October morning of gales and driving rain; the sort of day when spray and spindrift rise in wispy clouds from the surface of the sea lochs, when the mountainsides are streaked with running water, when hill burns overflow their courses, and when every tiny dip and hollow in the already saturated ground contains its own muddy pool or puddle. The wind is wrenching the leaves from the birch trees beside the Highbridge road. Mist shrouds the upper slopes of Aonach Mor which a recently established ski company has been trying unilaterally to rechristen Nevis Range. In a field beside a quarry which doubles as a local authority rubbish tip a flock of herring gulls have given up their scavenging in order to seek some shelter from the rising storm.

On a not dissimilar day some forty years ago, at a time when the newspapers and the radio bulletins were full of the police search for the Scottish students who had so audaciously taken the Stone of Destiny from London, there came to this part of the West Highlands a man called Calum MacLean; a man in search of the history and lore of the place. In the little crofting township of Highbridge, its diminutive holdings carved from previously barren moorland in order to provide a convenient receptacle for the victims of nineteenth-century evictions, Calum MacLean, as he afterwards recalled, found what he was looking for.

'It was on a Sunday morning in January 1951 that I first met little John Macdonald of Highbridge or John the Bard, as he is called. He had just come from Mass in the church at Roy Bridge. That morning he had cycled over eight miles to church through showers of sleet and hail. That was not bad for a man of seventy-five years of age. He wore no overcoat. John Macdonald is a sturdy man, somewhat under medium height, but very alert and active. His little grey eyes seemed to pierce right through me as I approached him.

'I greeted him in Gaelic. On hearing his own language, he immediately shed his reserve and smiled. He was John the Bard. He could not remember how many songs he had composed, perhaps a hundred or two. He had just composed a song in praise of the young Scots who removed the Stone of Destiny from Westminster Abbey. The Stone was then at large. We crouched down behind a wall and he sang the song. It was full of vigour and fire. The historic Scottish nation still lived. The Stone of Destiny really belonged to Scotland. John the Bard did not give a damn if the police never set eyes on it again. Of course he would tell me stories. His father knew everything that ever happened in Lochaber. He would meet me that afternoon. He sprang up, mounted his cycle with the agility of a youth of seventeen and was gone. I knew I had met a real character.'

Calum MacLean – though born on a Raasay croft rather than in an Islay mansion – was a folklorist very much in the tradition of John Francis Campbell. The brother of Sorley MacLean, one of the greatest Gaelic poets of this or any other century, the uncle of Cailean MacLean whose photographs illustrate these pages, the more distant kinsman of Jim MacLeod of Coeur d'Alene, North Idaho, with whose search for his Scottish Highland origins this book began, Calum, having obtained a first-class honours degree in Celtic languages at Edinburgh University, went on to win a postgraduate scholarship which enabled him to pursue his linguistic studies in University College, Dublin.

Ireland had much the same effect on Calum MacLean as it had earlier had on John Murdoch. It confirmed him in his commitment to things Gaelic. He became a Catholic. He made himself fluent in the Irish version of his native tongue. Moving from Dublin to Connemara, he began sytematically to collect local tradition. Soon he was on the staff of the Irish Folklore Commission which, shortly after Ireland had won its independence in 1921, the Dublin administration had established with a view to preserving as much as possible of the country's Gaelic heritage. It was as an employee of this Irish government agency – which was much more interested in the traditions of the Highlands and Islands than any comparable British institution – that Calum MacLean came back to Scotland in the years immediately after the Second World War.

Using early sound recording machines rather than the paper and pencil with

JOHN MACDONALD'S FORMER HOUSE, HIGHBRIDGE, LOCHABER

which John Francis Campbell had had to make do, MacLean – who was to die of cancer at the tragically early age of 45 – became a familiar figure in places like Lochaber. The people with whom he spent his time there were not persons of much social standing: fishermen, crofters, shepherds, roadmen, tinkers. But for all their lowly status, such men and women – and John the Bard of Highbridge was by no means untypical of them – clearly seemed to Calum MacLean an aristocracy more prestigious by far than the anglicised and titled landed gentry in their castles and big houses. For it was among the commonalty, among John Macdonald and his like, that there lingered the best features of the Gaelic civilisation which authority had so long been trying to obliterate.

In their efforts to eradicate what had gone before in the Highlands and Islands, eighteenth and nineteenth-century British governments had enjoyed the unstinting backing of the various Presbyterian churches whose clergymen were almost unanimously of the opinion that Gaelic lore was, at best, a diversion from matters of proper spiritual concern and, at worst, a repository of those superstitious, even Popish, practices which, the Protestant clerics thought, far too many Gaels – in defiance of Reformation principle – had so infuriatingly shown no great desire to set aside.

Raasay, where Calum MacLean grew up, was and still is a predominantly Free Presbyterian island. And the Free Presbyterians are one of the more strict Protestant denominations – refusing, as MacLean himself wrote, even to admit to the Communion sacrament those individuals who are considered to have infringed the little sect's extraordinarily unforgiving moral code.

'Before the minister calls the devout to communicate, he proceeds to indicate the categories that are to be debarred from partaking of the Lord's Supper. Relevant passages from the Bible are read, passages denouncing idolaters, adulterers, usurers, murderers, pilferers and so forth. Before he finishes he has practically succeeded in debarring the whole congregation. The sheep are then separated from the goats and the goats are very numerous. But among the goats there are people who tell stories about Fionn and Oisean, people who sing lovely songs like *Braigh Rusgaich*, those who love a pibroch like *MacCrimmon's Sweetheart*, those who can dance the *Highland Schottische* all night long and still go on, those who love to watch a good game of shinty and those who will continue to get gloriously drunk at weddings and at New Year. And they remain unrepentant.'

From the crofting township which was once home to John the Bard, I drive eastward to Spean Bridge where the approach to the village is dominated nowadays by the towering, bright red sign that stands outside the Little Chef restaurant on the community's southern outskirts. Crossing the river, I turn into Glen Spean and make for Cille Choirill. This is the church which bears the name of an Irish monk who came here to Brae Lochaber, most probably by way of Iona, shortly after St Columba's time. Long roofless, it has been twice restored this century. And because Brae Lochaber is one link in the long chain of Highlands and Islands localities – starting in the west in Barra and the Uists and ending in the east in places like Glen Livet and Upper Deeside – where a Romanised version of Columba's faith survived the sixteenth-century Scottish Reformation, Cille Choirill is a Catholic place of worship.

It is dark and cold inside the church this sunless morning. There is a constant noise of wind. The rain batters intermittently on the slated roof. I sit in one of the narrow wooden pews and look in the direction of the plain little altar with its row of candles. I am myself, as I have previously remarked, a Protestant and Protestants – Scottish Protestants anyway – are warned sternly to avoid the Catholic practice of offering up prayers for the souls of people who are dead. But here in Cille Choirill – which I know the man sometimes visited – I can see nothing wrong with risking a word on behalf of the Catholic convert, Calum MacLean, from whom, I suspect, God Himself and all His angels are likely to have heard a Gaelic song or two by now. After all, if there is indeed an afterworld presided over by the Galilean carpenter who once changed water into wine to let a Canaan wedding go ahead in the way that any wedding should, it is bound to have a corner – kept deliberately free of sour, hard-faced, black-hatted Calvinist preachers of the Hebridean type – where the likes of Calum MacLean can share a dram and listen to a tale.

In a Roy Bridge pub where three stormbound anglers are discussing fishing prospects in voices so loud as to mark them out immediately as belonging to that endlessly assertive class of English sportsmen who have constituted one of the less appealing features of the Highland scene for a hundred years or more, I sip a glass of beer, dry off my dripping anorak, and glance through the little booklet which I picked up at Cille Choirill. The booklet provides visitors with all the information which can be discovered now about the church and its surrounding graveyard, where the folk of Brae Lochaber have been buried for as long as anyone can remember. Its principal author is Ann MacDonell and that afternoon I call on her.

Ann was raised on a nearby croft in the depression years of the 1930s, when the Blackface lambs on which crofters relied for much of their livelihood were changing hands for no more than a few shillings, and when her mother and father, in order to earn the cash needed for – among many other things – their daughter's education, were obliged to let out practically every room in their croft house to the families of the navvies and tradesmen who were then employed on the dams and power stations built hereabouts just prior to the Second World War in order to provide the British Aluminium Company's Fort William smelter with its necessary supplies of hydro-electricity.

'The one thing I made up my mind about when I was still a girl,' Ann tells me with great emphasis, 'was that, whatever else I did, I was not going to spend my life on a croft.'

In fact, she became a primary school teacher. Now, in her retirement, she has made herself a leading local historian and genealogist; the sort of person who is invariably sought out by the many Americans, Canadians, Australians, New Zealanders and others who – in the manner of Jim MacLeod from Idaho – come each year to the Highlands and Islands with a view to discovering the now long-abandoned settlements which their ancestors were forced to leave at the time of the clearances.

I ask Ann what it means to men and women of that sort to find the precise spot where their people used to live. 'You have no idea how important it is to them,' she says, 'no idea. Often there are tears in their eyes.

'There was one man who came to my house here. MacMillan was his name. He was a Canadian. And, because he had no car, I took him myself to Loch Arkaig side, to the very place where we'd established that his family stayed all these years ago. Well, he just sat there and wept and wept.

'People are tremendously touched by this feeling of getting back to where their forebears once belonged. You see them all the time in summer up there at Cille Choirill. They sit in the church and think of their ancestors sitting there. They look at the hills and think of their ancestors looking at the same hills, one hundred, two hundred, three hundred years ago.'

Ann MacDonell compares this rediscovering of one's origins to the feeling that a salmon must experience when, after it has swum the greater part of the Atlantic Ocean, it finally gets the scent of its own West Highland river; the river where, for that fish, everything began. These people, these Canadians, these Americans, she says, have long since made their lives elsewhere. And most of them, Ann stresses, have done very well. But they still, to her mind anyway, have a little bit of the homecoming salmon about them. They know that somehow this remains their place.

Not surprisingly, then, the most recent restoration of Cille Choirill, completed in 1987, was partially financed by dollars collected by North American descendants of Brae Lochaber folk, this overseas fund-raising effort being concentrated in the many Nova Scotia and Cape Breton Island communities which still bear the mark of their West Highland origins.

The Lochaber man who made the journey to Canada to collect this money was a friend of mine, Ronnie Campbell, a Glen Roy crofter whom I got to know in the middle part of the 1980s when I was involved with Ronnie and many others in putting together the organisation which eventually became known as the Scottish Crofters Union.

Now, in the late afternoon of the day which began at Highbridge and with a welcome glint of sunshine lighting up the autumn colours of the birches in the vicinity of Ronnie's home at Bohuntin, we are making our way together up the road which runs parallel to the heavily swollen waters of the River Roy and stopping every now and then to take in some particular historical detail of the kind known only to those – such as Ronnie Campbell – who have access to those bits of purely local information which come down by word of mouth from one generation to the next.

We pause, first of all, at one of Brae Lochaber's several mass stones – the name given to those lumps of rock pressed into service as makeshift altars in the penal times of the seventeenth and eighteenth centuries when to be a Roman Catholic in Scotland was to be permanently at odds with the law and when mass was necessarily celebrated on this open Brae Lochaber hillside by priests and people constantly at risk of arrest, or worse, at the hands of military patrols whose job it was to stamp out Highland Popery.

Ronnie mentions how a fugitive Earl of Mar, fleeing Lochaber after the destruction of his army by the forces of the Lordship of the Isles in 1431, was assisted by a Glen Roy man called Cameron; how James IV, on one of his several Highland journeys, spent a night somewhere in this vicinity; how, in the summer of 1932, Bishop Alexander MacDonald of Victoria, British Columbia, who had come to Scotland to preach at Cille Choirill, was able to find – as a result of the precise directions he had been given as a small boy by his grandmother – the well which had traditionally served a long gone Glen Roy township.

It was from Glen Roy that Ronnie Campbell's own great-great-great-great-grandfather, Ewen MacIntosh, *Eoghann Ruadh*, left to fight with Prince Charles Edward Stuart's army in 1745 – going eventually to his final resting place at Cille Choirill with an English musket ball still lodged firmly in his shoulder. And it was from Glen Roy that Ewen's son, Donald, the brother of Ronnie's great-great-great-grandfather, set off to serve with General James Wolfe in that later eighteenth-century campaign which finally established British rule in Canada.

Here, not far short short of a recently renovated nineteenth-century shooting lodge where the waters of the Turret merge with those of the Roy, is the shattered stump of the pine tree from which, at the beginning of February 1645, that greatest of all MacDonald warriors, Alasdair MacColla, is said to have threatened to hang the Brae Lochaber bard, *Iain Lom*, if the army then being led down the glen by MacColla and the Marquis of Montrose should find the disposition of the forces being arrayed against MacColla by the Earl of Argyll to be anything other than the way the bard had described it to him.

Not far away, at a place which Glen Roy people call the Briagach, formerly a settlement but now no more than a set of steeply sloping fields across which Ronnie and I walk in yet another squall of rain, is an odd-shaped boulder. Mostly it consists of granite, but round its middle runs a belt of slightly softer, rougher rock. Here, so the young Ronnie Campbell was informed matter-of-

ANN MACDONELL OF SPEAN BRIDGE

127

factly by his father one day when the two of them were attending to the Bohuntin sheep stock, a number of Montrose's soldiers – pausing briefly to snatch some shelter and some hospitality in those homes whose ruins are still to be seen nearby – sharpened their swords in preparation for the battle which they knew would very soon be joined.

The route taken by Montrose and MacColla in the course of their forced march through these parts is one with which Ronnie Campbell is more familiar than any man alive. As one of his many contributions to the fund-raising effort launched in connection with Cille Choirill's reconstruction, he led a party of fifteen men in a sponsored re-enactment of it; insisting on making the trip from the southern end of Loch Ness through the high hills between Glen Buck and Glen Turret and on through Caol Lairig to Corriechoille and Inverlochy, as the men of 1645 had done, in the depths of winter; fording an ice-fringed River Spean; bivouacking only briefly in the middle of the long winter's night; accomplishing the entire march of nearly forty miles, as Montrose and MacColla are known to have accomplished it, in under twenty-four hours.

'We were lucky with the weather,' Ronnie says modestly when I tell him that this journey was no small achievement.

'We were always lucky with the weather when Cille Choirill was being rebuilt,' Ann MacDonell had told me earlier. 'Everything from Ronnie's walk to the actual work done on the site seemed to take place in conditions that were little short of perfect.' The saints of the Columban Church, it seems, are not without their influence in high places yet.

When, in the 1640s, England, Scotland and Ireland became inextricably entangled in the civil wars, rebellions and revolutions that were to end, following the eventual execution of Charles I, in Oliver Cromwell's imposing his own brand of personal rule on every part of the British Isles, all sorts of opportunities were presented to those who wished to advance the interests of previously disadvantaged sectors of the population.

Presbyterian extremists known as Covenanters – people who had been theologically and politically marginalised in the course of Charles's efforts to impose a much more Episcopalian form of Church government on his Scottish kingdom – seized power in the Lowlands. In England – where a Parliament representing mainly businessmen and landowners found that, in seeking to wrest authority from the monarchy, it had stirred up new and potentially explosive aspirations among the poor – there were demands for every working man to have the vote. Meanwhile, the various troubles on the British mainland

LIATHACH FROM ACHNASHEEN, ROSS-SHIRE

COLDBACKIE, SUTHERLAND

ELPHIN, SUTHERLAND

LUSKENTYRE, ISLE OF HARRIS

SUNSET FROM THE WEST SIDE OF MULL

AN OAK AT ARIUNDLE

AUTUMN

GLEN ROY IN AUTUMN

THE ROOT SYSTEM OF AN ANCIENT TREE, REVEALED BY EROSION

PORT NA CURAICH, IONA

WAVES BREAKING ON THE WEST COAST OF UIST

POL A CHARRA, SOUTH UIST

were inevitably interpreted in Ireland to mean that the time had come to mount yet another bid to be free of English rule.

It was not at all surprising, then, that many Highlanders should promptly have embroiled themselves in the general convulsion with a view to undoing the effects of the assault which the Stewart monarchy had for some time been mounting on their society and its institutions. But it was more than a little ironic – in view of the rôle which his family had played in the destruction of the Lordship of the Isles and the promulgation of so many measures of the type imposed on clan chieftains by the Statutes of Iona – that those Gaels who most explicitly saw themselves as seeking to restore a less repressive order in their corner of Britain should have chosen to intervene in the wider political struggle on the side of Charles I.

Charles's own opinion of Highlanders had initially been every bit as unfavourable as that of his father, James VI. In 1626 he had urged his Scottish ministers to have an English-language school erected at once in every Highlands and Islands parish 'for the better civilising' of the north of Scotland population. In 1630, in anticipation of a course of action which was actually to be implemented by the evicting landlords of a later period, he had gone so far as to contemplate the wholesale removal of that population to Nova Scotia. By the early 1640s, however, the increasingly embattled king was having to take his allies where he found them; not least among the previously despised Gaelic-speaking peoples of Ireland and the Scottish Highlands.

Thus there began to be forged that much-romanticised alliance between a significant proportion of the Highland clans, on the one side, and, on the other, the royal house of Stewart – or Stuart as the family name was more commonly rendered by the later, and increasingly Francophile, descendants of that Breton immigrant of so many centuries before.

The long-term effects of this alignment, of course, were to be disastrous for the Scottish Highlands. Those Englishmen, Scots and Irishmen who favoured the Stuart cause were not necessarily the died-in-the-wool reactionaries of later legend; just as those who lined up against the Stuarts – the more determinedly obscurantist Covenanters, for example – were by no means invariably on the side of enlightenment and democracy as we should understand these things. But there was undoubtedly a very broad sense in which the Stuarts – believing, as they did, in their supposedly divine right to rule – stood for forces which were destined to lose out historically. And because the Gaels identified themselves so strongly with the Stuart cause, they made it all the more certain that, when that cause finally went down to total defeat, their own traditional society would be even more harshly treated by the men with whom the future lay than might otherwise have been the case.

Little of this, admittedly, was readily foreseeable in the 1640s. Then, from the perspective of those West Highland and Hebridean clans which were to take the lead in what was soon to follow, only two things were clear. One was that the Covenanting régime which had installed itself in Edinburgh was not likely to look with favour on their own continuing predilection for Episcopalianism or Catholicism. The other was that a leading light in that régime was none other than the Earl of Argyll, MacCailein Mor, chief of the Inveraray Campbells and a man who, for all that imminent events were to cast some doubt on his courage, possessed in full measure those qualities of political acumen and insight which, over so long a period, enabled his clan to emerge from successive upheavals with its political influence strengthened and enhanced.

Those Gaels who now went to war on the side of King Charles, it seems likely, were motivated not so much by a sudden onrush of royalism as by their longstanding hatred of MacCailein Mor and all his kin. This was certainly true of that most outstanding soldier in whose footsteps Ronnie Campbell – his own surname, as he takes care to inform me, deriving from a segment of his clan which has long been settled in Brae Lochaber and which, accordingly, tended to be both Catholic and Jacobite in outlook – was to make his own march through Glen Roy.

Alasdair MacColla – so called because he was a son of Colla Ciotach of Colonsay – is identified primarily with that branch of Clan Donald which, in the era of the lordship, had established itself in Antrim. This was not so much a reversal of the Dalriadan settlement of a thousand years before as an especially striking demonstration of the exent to which both Ireland and the Highlands and Islands were still seen to constitute a single cultural entity. And for all that Alasdair himself is sometimes categorised as Irish, it makes more sense to think of him as a MacDonald whose primary mission it was to restore his kindred to its former greatness and, in the process, to eject the Campbells from those territories – most notably Islay and Kintyre – which had been the source of so much of the power once wielded so effectively by the MacDonald Lords of the Isles.

This, for certain, was how Alasdair MacColla was regarded by the Brae Lochaber bard, John MacDonald, Iain Lom – the man whom, when the two met in the upper reaches of Glen Roy that February day in 1645, MacColla is said to have threatened to string up on the tree shown to me by Ronnie Campbell if the poet, whose bones now lie in the Cille Choirill graveyard,

THE CHURCHYARD OF CILLE CHOIRILL

should be found to be dealing in deliberately misleading intelligence as to the precise whereabouts of MacColla's Campbell and Covenanter opponents.

But there was no Highlander whose loyalties need have troubled Alasdair less than those of Iain Lom whose desire to have Clan Campbell deprived of what he called the green and lovely lands of Islay and Kintyre was every bit as strong as MacColla's own.

From Iain Lom's verses MacColla emerges as a 'spirited princely youth who would rouse thousands'; a man uniquely skilled in the use of his basket-hilted sword 'with its cleaving sharp blue edge of steel'; a man who, more than any other, was possessed of the vision and the bravery needed to win again for Clan Donald its headship of the Gael. Some part of these resounding tributes can perhaps be dismissed as bardic exaggeration of the standard kind. But there is much of what was said by Iain Lom – the last traces of whose home can just be seen by the roadside in the long emptied countryside a little to the east of the modern Laggan Dam – which has to it the ring of simple truth. Alasdair MacColla was clearly an impressive man.

MacColla's first encounters with MacCailein Mor took place in Ireland where the Earl of Argyll had been sent by Scotland's Covenanter government in order to offer some military assistance to Ulster's Protestant settlers who were increasingly at risk from those rebellious Irishmen with whom MacColla, after some initial prevarication, had thrown in his lot. But it was in Scotland that MacColla was to win his long enduring fame among the Gaels. In July 1644 he sailed from Ireland to Morvern at the head of an expeditionary force consisting of both Irishmen and Scots, the latter being mainly MacLean and MacDonald refugees from Campbell persecution. The main Campbell strongholds in Morvern and Ardnamurchan were quickly taken, MacColla subsequently marching north into Kintail and then southward into the Great Glen, Badenoch and Atholl, endeavouring to rally Highlanders to the cause of King Charles and Clan Donald.

What would have come of this campaign of rapid movement and occasional military success had MacColla been left entirely to his own devices, it is impossible to say. For in Atholl at the very moment, it is said, when MacColla was actually praying for divine guidance as to how he might more productively confront his foes, there came up to him three men on horseback, one of whom introduced himself as James Graham, Marquis of Montrose.

Montrose, who had begun the civil war as a Covenanter but who had gone on to become King Charles's supreme commander in Scotland, was – prior to his dramatic encounter with Alasdair MacColla – a general without an army; MacColla, for his part, had previously been all too easily dismissed, particularly by the more influential and respectable Scottish loyalists whose backing he had hoped to gain, as a rash and more than slightly disreputable adventurer who, for all that he might appeal to the wild men of the West Highland hills, could not be said to be the sort of company that any self-respecting gentleman would want to keep.

The two soldiers, in short, needed each other. And their dramatic meeting on the Braes of Atholl accordingly proved the prelude to one of the more remarkable military campaigns ever experienced in Scotland; a campaign, moreover, which had the effect of once again making Highlanders – substantial numbers of whom now threw in their lot with MacColla and Montrose – a potentially decisive element in the wider Scottish scene.

At Tippermuir, near Perth, at the beginning of September 1644, for the first time since the men of the Lordship of the Isles had confronted the Earl of Mar some two hundred years before, Gaels engaged in a pitched battle with forces raised by Scotland's central government. And the day, this time, belonged without doubt to the Highlanders. The Covenanting army commanded by Lord Elcho (and carrying on its banners the chilling Covenanter slogan of 'Jesus and no quarter') was effectively annihilated – as five more such armies were to be in the six months ahead.

Alasdair's great contribution to these victories was to have grasped the tactical possibilities inherent in a Highland army equipped with lightweight weaponry of the sort then becoming widely available in Scotland. The gallow-glasses and their like had worn cumbersome body armour and had armed themselves with enormously heavy two-handed swords and axes. Their fighting prowess was indisputable, but they lacked mobility, and MacColla's genius, like that of Montrose, lay in the art of the lightning attack: the sudden, racing, screaming, devastating onslaught which, for all that its practitioners might lack the finer points of military discipline, was repeatedly proved capable – through-out the hundred years which separated Alasdair MacColla from Prince Charles Edward Stuart – of carrying all before it.

The great sword of the past was now no more. Its place had been taken by what the bards called *lann Spainnteach*, the Spanish or Toledo blade, the flexible and singlehanded weapon which Iain Lom explicitly associates with MacColla himself; and on which MacColla's Highland troops – like those belonging to the Jacobite armies of subsequent decades – certainly relied. Combined with the protection afforded to a charging man by his equally portable leather targe or shield, and the further offensive capability supplied by the dirk or dagger employed in the close-quarter skirmishing which followed his initial and usually shattering onslaught, this new and singlehanded sword made of the Highland soldier a truly formidable foe.

Highlanders also carried muskets. But having loosed off a scattered volley at the start of an engagement, they tended, as was observed by the English soldier Henry Hawley, who was himself on the receiving end of a Highland charge in the course of the last Jacobite rebellion, to throw their muskets to one side and hurl themselves forwards. As they charged, wrote Hawley, the conventional battle lines in which they had originally been drawn up gave way to tightly packed bunches of men: 'separate bands, like wedges, condensed and firm'. Such a charge could be deflected, Hawley considered and as Culloden was to prove, if the defenders held their fire until the Highlanders were practically on top of them. But this, of course, demanded almost superhuman self-control. The typical English or Lowland infantryman was inclined to discharge his first round when the Highlanders were still some way off; and if he did, Hawley warned, he would not get a chance to fire again.

'If fire is given at a distance,' Henry Hawley told his soldiers, 'you will probably be broke; for you never get time to load a second cartridge.' And the commanding officer who gave ground in such a battle, the Englishman added, might as well give up his troops for dead. The Highlanders, as Hawley put it, 'being without a firelock or any load, no man with his arms and accoutrements can escape them; and they give no quarter.'

From the other side of the increasingly embittered north-south divide, the Jacobite poet, Aonghas MacAlasdair, insisting – with all the wisdom of a survivor of the Battle of Killiecrankie and the subsequent rising of 1715 – that no army, however formidable, was unbeatable by Highlanders, urged on his fellow Gaels in terms which Henry Hawley would have recognised as the mirror image of his own account of Highland tactics.

'Do not let the sound of gunpowder put the slightest anxiety into your bodies, nor blue-black muskets cause any decline in your hopes; whenever that sound dies away, your distress and hurt are at an end; you will be tackling them at close quarters according to your time-honoured practice.'

The growing availability of field artillery, fire-holding techniques of the type advocated by Hawley and, above all, the development of the bayonet, were eventually to enable regular British troops to counter the Highland charge. But they were a long time coming. The Highlanders who, in 1689, flowed down that Killiecrankie hillside, as one awestruck watcher afterwards noted, 'like a living flood'; the Highlanders who, as Daniel Defoe observed, were not only 'wonderfully swift of foot' but seemingly more capable than any other race of enduring 'cold, hunger and hardship'; the Highlanders who could march twenty, thirty or even more miles in a single day with no more sustenance than that provided by a handful of oatmeal mixed with water; these were men who, in the hands of a general of Alasdair MacColla's stamp, seemed capable of performing miracles.

But for all MacColla's brilliant innovations, one thing had not changed with the passing of the centuries. The trumpets which the Roman Empire's Celtic adversaries had so frighteningly blown before the commencement of their attacks might have given way to the still more disconcerting sound of the bagpipe – that most warlike of instruments which, in the course of the six-teenth century, had begun to supersede the harp throughout the Scottish Highlands. But the war-cries which Caesar's legionaries had found so demora-lising in the Gaul or Britain of nearly two thousand years before were still a key component of the Highland approach to making war. Nor did MacColla's men deal simply in repeated shouts and screams. The giving of a Highland battle-cry, it seems, was a highly specialised vocal art, one which it is now impossible to reproduce with any certainty. But whatever a Gaelic war-cry sounded like, there is no doubt as to its purpose. It was designed to terrify an enemy; and from another conflict in another century on another continent there comes this eloquent testimony to its effect.

'There is nothing like it on this side of the infernal region,' recalled a northern veteran of America's civil war. 'The peculiar corkscrew sensation that it sends down your backbone … can never be told. You have to feel it.'

That man was speaking of the so-called 'rebel yell', that 'strange and eerie scream' first heard to emanate from the victorious Confederate army at the Battle of Bull Run in July 1861. Precisely where Robert E. Lee's southern soldiers picked up the 'unearthly wail' that they were soon to make their trademark is still in dispute, but by no means the least implausible account of its origins attributes the rebel yell to troops from the Carolinas: troops with Scottish Highland names who were descended from the many Gaels who settled in these parts in the eighteenth century.

RONNIE CAMPBELL OF GLEN ROY

From Perth MacColla and Montrose swung north into the Angus and Aberdeenshire Lowlands: again defeating the Covenanters, taking Aberdeen itself. A fresh force, commanded by none other than the Earl of Argyll, was put into the field against them. Their own army was now divided in two: Montrose remained in the east while Alasdair swung westward into Ardnamurchan, raising the Campbell sieges of those castles he had seized on first coming to Scotland, and foregathering with Montrose once more in Atholl.

Now it was November, the time when armies then were expected to take to winter quarters and await the spring. But neither Montrose nor Alasdair was a conventional soldier. 'I was willing to let the world see that Argyll was not the man his Highlandmen believed him to be and that it was possible to beat him in his own Highlands,' Montrose informed Charles I by letter. So commenced a brutally effective invasion of the Campbell heartland.

'Throughout all Argyll,' runs an account of the subsequent campaign which was sent at the time to Ireland and which was possibly penned by Alasdair MacColla, 'we left neither house nor hold unburned, nor corn nor cattle, that belonged to the whole name of Campbell.' MacCailein Mor himself was forced to flee from the advancing MacDonalds. Mass was defiantly said again in Protestant Argyll. By mid-winter, it was reported, no cock was to be heard crowing and no chimney could be seen smoking within twenty miles of Inveraray. For years afterwards there would be no more dreaded name among the Campbells than that of Alasdair MacColla – *fear tholtaidh nan tighean*, the destroyer of homes.

Northward the army now marched into Appin and Duror where, since MacColla and Montrose were again in the lands of clans – in this instance the Stewarts – who had long felt themselves threatened by the Campbells, another 150 men were recruited.

North still they went into Lochaber, keeping to the eastern shore of Loch Linnhe, entering the Great Glen and skirting Loch Lochy and Loch Oich; pausing eventually at the southern end of Loch Ness where the British military would one day establish a garrison called Fort Augustus.

Montrose and MacColla now had some two thousand men at their disposal. But ahead of them, in the neighbourhood of Inverness, was yet another Covenanting force with more than double their strength. And behind them, in the vicinity of Inverlochy, where Cromwell's troops would shortly construct the strongpoint to be known eventually as Fort William, was the further army, at least three thousand strong, which had been raised by a vengeful Earl of Argyll.

The Great Glen, as it had been since the time of Colum Cille, who came this way on his journeyings to the kingdom of the Picts, is a natural thoroughfare. But in winter – and it was now late in January – it is also a trap. The few high passes on either side of the valley are usually so deep in snow as to have made it seem unlikely to Argyll and the Covenanters that Montrose and Alasdair could do anything other than remain within the confines of the Great Glen itself.

But the earl had again failed to comprehend the quality of the men he was pursuing. Following the route which Ronnie Campbell and his companions were to take more than three centuries later, MacColla and Montrose struck boldy into the hills – to emerge, before Argyll had properly grasped what had happened, on the slopes above the castle of Inverlochy; slopes now occupied by the British Aluminium Company's smelter complex and the outer suburban sprawl of modern Fort William.

On the wings of their little army, they placed the troops MacColla had brought from Ireland. In the centre were the Stewarts of Appin and Atholl, the MacDonalds of Glencoe and the men of Lochaber – some three hundred Camerons prominent among them. Only a little to the rear, constituting a second line of attack, were the Clanranald MacDonalds, the MacDonalds of Keppoch and the MacLean chiefs of Duart, Coll, Kinlochaline, Treshnish and Ardgour.

At Inverlochy, as many of these men would have heard from their bards, the MacDonald Lords of the Isles had defeated the forces of the Scottish Crown in 1431. Now, more than two hundred years later, in the opinion at least of Iain Lom, who personally witnessed the unfolding of events this February Sunday morning in 1645, Clan Donald was to show that, for all the defeats and disappointments of the intervening period, it was still capable of greatness.

Argyll's Lowland infantry once more fled in the face of a Highland charge. The earl's Campbell clansmen did little better, falling and dying in their hundreds on the flat land surrounding the mouth of the River Lochy. Again MacCailein Mor was put to ignominious flight, taking to his waiting galley and sailing off down Loch Linnhe while the men of his beaten army were still being slaughtered on the shore.

'I climbed early on Sunday morning to the brae above Inverlochy Castle,' exulted Iain Lom. 'I saw the army taking up position and victory lay with Clan Donald.'

This was the day of Alasdair, the bard declaimed, the day of Alasdair 'of the sharp biting blades', the day of Alasdair, 'son of handsome Colla'.

'You remember the place called the Tawny Field? It got a fine dose of manure; not the dung of sheep or goats, but Campbell blood well congealed. To hell with you if I care for your plight, as I listen to your children's distress, lamenting the band that went to battle, the howling of the women of Argyll.'

There would be other victories for Montrose and Alasdair MacColla, at Auldearn, at Alford and at Kilsyth. Argyll would be occupied a second time; even Kintyre would be briefly controlled once more by the MacDonalds. But for all the tactical brilliance they displayed, Montrose and MacColla, like all the various Jacobite commanders who came after them, were incapable of solving the most fundamental of the many problems confronting those who sought to change the course of Scottish or British history from an essentially Highlands and Islands power base.

Not for many generations had it proved possible for Gaels to impose their will on the country they called Alba, still less on the much larger entity which, by the time of Montrose and MacColla, was beginning to be named Great Britain. Long gone were the days when a man like Colum Cille, operating from a little island in Dalriada, could aspire to shape the pattern of events over territories stretching all the way to the Humber. The social, cultural, political and economic forces which were now moving things along – and moving them also at an ever faster pace – in the wider society to the south and east of the Highland Line were too strong for Highlanders alone to combat with any real prospect of long-term success.

Montrose and MacColla had looked for support beyond the Highlands. They did not find it. And so they were ultimately to fail in their objectives, Montrose eventually being executed in Scotland and MacColla dying in battle against the English in the south of Ireland.

The same pattern – of an essentially Highland rising gaining initial, and often striking, military success only for the rebels sooner or later to run headlong into a wall of southern indifference or hostility – was to be repeated, over and over again, in the years ahead.

When the Stuarts, having been restored on Cromwell's death only to be expelled again in 1688, looked once more to Highlanders for their salvation, there was no lack of enthusiasm among those whom nineteenth and twentieth-century sentimentalists would dub the loyal clans. But for all that their leader on that occasion, Graham of Claverhouse, *Iain Dubh nan Cath*, Black John of the Battles, had more than a dash of the Montrose about him, he proved no more able than his predecessor of forty years before to instil in Lowlanders any affection for a royal house which had proved so congenitally incapable of measuring up to the challenges of the times.

Again the Highlanders were defeated; as they were in 1715 and 1719; as they were to be, most crushingly of all, at the conclusion, in April 1746, of *bliadhna Thearlaich* – the twelve months, as the Gaelic bards put it, which belonged to Charles Edward Stuart.

Steadily, endlessly, inexorably, the old Highland order had been drawing to a close over the hundred years which separated MacColla's triumph at Inverlochy from the disaster of Culloden. Scotland had united with England in 1707. A new dynasty of kings had been imported from Hanover to guarantee the supremacy of both Parliament and Protestantism. Towns like Glasgow were beginning to expand enormously. The first factories were appearing. A huge new empire was being developed in India and North America. And it was most implausible, to put it mildly, that the world's first industrial nation – a country then vying with France for global supremacy – was forever going to tolerate within its frontiers the continuation of the still Gaelic-speaking, still semi-autonomous, still massively divergent society of the Scottish Highlands.

Cromwell's General Monck and the Hanoverian monarchy's General Wade constructed modern roads and modern fortifications in the strategic centre of the mainland Highlands. The MacDonalds of Glencoe were massacred – with the same sort of ruthlessness which later British governments would one day show in their dealings with other restless hill tribes far away – as a deliberate act of state policy. More amenable Highlanders – the men of the so-called Black Watch – began to be recruited into the British military apparatus, their main initial task being to give some protection to the rapidly expanding cattle trade which was itself helping to turn the thoughts of more and more Highland chieftains towards new, more commercial and less warlike, means of sustaining their prestige.

Thus it came about that when the French government, by way of adding to the difficulties of their British adversaries in the course of the much wider conflict known as the War of the Austrian Succession, hit on the expedient of conveying the latest Stuart hopeful to the Hebrides in the summer of 1745, there was no overwhelming rush to the Jacobite standard which Prince Charles Edward unfurled at Glenfinnan.

But for all that only a fraction of the military potential of the Highlands and Islands was ever mobilised on behalf of the somewhat ineffectual individual known to a thousand balladeers as Bonnie Prince Charlie, still there were men prepared to risk everything for the Jacobite cause. Partly they went to war – as

GLEN ROY IN LOCHABER

many others have done since – because they were compelled to do so; by their chiefs, on this occasion, rather than by the conscription authorities of later times. Partly they fought on behalf of the Episcopalian and Catholic faiths which Lowland Presbyterians had not yet succeeded in extinguishing in much of the north. Partly they were motivated by nationalistic dislike of the Union which bards like Iain Lom so ferociously condemned. Partly they wanted to strike another blow against the Campbells who, as always, were on the side of central government. Partly, no doubt, they felt some real residual affection for the Stuarts who, in spite of everything, still stood a great deal closer to the line of Alba's ancient kings than any Hanoverian ever could.

Nearly a full century after the Young Pretender's landing in Scotland, it would afterwards be recalled by a Glen Lyon man who was to leave a written account of his life and times, the coronation of Queen Victoria in 1838 had presented his aged and Gaelic-speaking grandmother with a welcome opportunity to rehearse the genealogy of Scotland's rulers. 'She and others of her generation enjoyed the liberty this occasion gave them for going ... to the history of the Scottish kings, as far as Kenneth MacAlpin, which had come down by oral tradition.' That tradition, we can be certain, was stronger still a hundred years before – when it must have helped to fuel Jacobitism.

But something else, something never very clearly stated, but something powerful all the same, seems to me to have underpinned the various other reasons for a man – such as the Strontian 'whiskie maker', John Cameron, whom we encountered in an earlier chapter – throwing in his lot with so manifestly hazardous an enterprise as yet another attempt to overthrow the British state by force of Highland arms. That something, I believe, was the conviction that whatever else the 1745 rising offered, it provided an opportunity – the last such opportunity as things turned out – to defend the integrity of the civilisation which had been implanted in Alba by the Gaels.

This, perhaps, was what inclined even so slippery and so unattractive a character as the Fraser chieftain, Lord Lovat, whose tortuous circumnavigations of the eighteenth-century political world led him finally into the Jacobite camp, to make it clear to his son – just prior to the father's beheading on a charge of treason – that of the several different languages in which he had conducted his life's business, Latin and Greek as well as French and English, it was Gaelic which he had come at last to value above all the rest.

What was true of the endlessly manoeuvring *MacShimidh*, it seems likely, was a good deal truer of those poets like Rob Donn MacKay or Duncan Ban MacIntyre who – though the one belonged to a pro-Hanoverian clan and though the other had actually fought against the Jacobites at the Battle of Falkirk in January 1746 – identified themselves so conspicuously in their verse with the cause of Charles Edward Stuart.

It is certainly no coincidence, I am certain, that Alasdair MacMhaighstir Alasdair – the Moidart and Ardnamurchan bard whose boyhood haunts I inspected in the course of my visit to my great-great-grandfather's home in Gleann na h-Iubraich – was both a passionate advocate of the cause of Gaelic and an enthusiastic officer in the Jacobite army of 1745.

For all that Gaelic was 'now struggling for its existence in a narrow corner', MacMhaighstir Alasdair wrote, for all that it had been for so long a victim of the 'great hatred' manifestly felt for it by those who were not Gaels, his 'mother tongue' had once been the language of kings and princes; the language of the people who had given shape to Scotland.

When such a man felt 'great joy and gladness' on hearing of Charles Edward Stuart's coming to his own 'land of Clanranald', when he made his way with all possible speed to Loch nan Uamh in Arisaig in order to be one of the first Highlanders to board the *Doutelle*, the French naval vessel which had brought Prince Charles to Scotland, he was not simply hoping to help replace one king in London with another. Alasdair MacMhaighstir Alasdair went to war in 1745 and 1746 for something much more fundamental, and – however naïve or mistaken men like Alasdair may subsequently have been thought – there were no doubt many like him.

Go to Culloden nowadays and you will find there a neatly landscaped carpark, an information centre, a souvenir store, a cafeteria and, at certain times of year, as many as several hundred visitors. This, though the place was less commercially developed then than now, was what most angered my father when, against his better judgment, he was prevailed upon to take my mother, my sister and myself here in the course of a trip we made to Inverness when I was still a boy. He had himself seen no small amount of military action in his time: at El Alamein; at Monte Cassino; at a dozen other places in North Africa, Sicily, Italy and Greece. That was no doubt why the notion of a battlefield having been turned into a tourist attraction clearly annoyed him not a little. He was manifestly disgusted with our bus tour courier's lighthearted chitchat. 'A lot of good men died here,' he said to us more than once.

Back at Culloden for the first time in thirty years, I remember that remark as I walk along the row of wooden plaques which mark the Jacobite front line. Here stood the Atholl brigade and here the Camerons; the Appin Stewarts;

Lovat's Frasers; the Farquharsons, the MacLeans, the Raasay MacLeods and the MacLachlans; the Chisholms; the Clanranald MacDonalds; those other MacDonalds of Keppoch and Glengarry. Somewhere here stood Eoghann Ruadh, great-great-great-great-grandfather to Ronnie Campbell of Glen Roy. Somewhere here, very possibly, stood men from whom I am myself descended one way or another.

They were cold, wet, bedraggled, hungry, exhausted and demoralised. They were not, however, the 'bare-arsed banditti' of Hanoverian propaganda. They had conquered all of Scotland. They had marched further into England than any Scottish army had ever done before. That they had not received in the south the popular backing which Charles Edward Stuart had promised them was not their fault. Nor was it any of their doing that the man for whom so many of them were to die that day had lied to their chiefs about the likelihood of French support; that he had amply demonstrated that his generalship was as flawed as so much of the rest of his character was speedily showing itself to be; that the criminal recklessness of the man was all too evident from the desperate plight in which his Highland soldiers found themselves that April morning.

He had brought them to battle, here on the outskirts of Inverness, in a place that was as high and flat and featureless as it was cold and windswept; a place where there was no possibility of their making the downhill charge which was now, as it had been since Alasdair MacColla first devised it, their most formidable tactic; a place where they stood – as it must have seemed to them for an entire age together – facing into a bitter gale of easterly wind; facing into squalls of sleet and hailstones; facing a withering fire of cannonball and grapeshot from the Duke of Cumberland's artillery.

Still they charged. For a full five hundred yards. Running, stumbling, falling. Minute after minute. Across ground soft and marshy; ground rough with ankle-snagging heather. In the damp and in the gunsmoke. The noise of their own harsh breathing drowned increasingly in screams and musket-fire. The smell of dirt and black powder and blood in their nostrils. Their friends and their neighbours being killed all around them. The sheer hopelessness of the enterprise clear to every one of them, by this time, as it had been clear for several hours past to the more able and intelligent of their officers; men whose advice Prince Charles Edward Stuart, with all the stupid, self-centred perversity which had long before cost his family their throne, had so casually and cavalierly disregarded.

Perhaps one and a half thousand of them eventually made contact with Cumberland's well-fed and well-clothed redcoats. Shouting still in their

Gaelic. Clambering over the mounting piles of their own dead. Their swords no match, it was all too amply demonstrated, for a triple-banked wall of bayonets wielded by men who understood now that this day was surely not to go to Highlanders.

They lie here still in their hundreds under the stones erected in the nineteenth century to their memory; the stones among which a scattering of end-of-season tourists are making their way on this autumn day of gusty wind and slowly clouding skies. There is the sound of traffic on the nearby road; the louder sound of a jet taking off from Inverness Airport. The world has long ago moved on and left Culloden's meaning – if it ever understood it – far behind.

That night, back home in Skye, I read again the words which, ever since I came across them in a book about North America's native peoples, have always seemed to me to encapsulate the fate of all those traditional societies whose misfortune it has been to get in the way of what history's winners invariably call progress.

'When I look back now from the high hill of my old age,' said Black Elk of the Oglala Sioux, remembering the white men's killing of his tribe, 'I can still see the butchered women and children lying heaped and scattered all along the crooked gulch as plain as when I saw them with eyes still young. And I can see that something else died there in the bloody mud and was buried in the blizzard. A people's dream died there. The nation's hoop is broken and scattered and the sacred tree is dead.'

CHAPTER EIGHT

On the summit of a rocky little knoll beside the road at the southern end of the Ballachulish Bridge, some three or four miles to the west of Glencoe, there is a small stone monument. Although the builders of the bridge provided both a lay-by and a flight of steps for such people as might wish to visit it, the hillock is so shrouded by trees and bracken, especially in July and August when the Highland tourist trade is at its most frenzied, that not very many people stop here. On a warm summer's evening, for all the noise of cars and lorries on the road below, this seems today a peaceful and secluded sort of spot.

But come here in the back end of the year, on one of those wild, dark and depressing days when the mist eddies back and forth among the peaks of Beinn a'Bheithir and the slanting sheets of rain are lashed along by a south-westerly gale; come here on such a day, when the last of the leaves have been stripped from the birches and the bracken has died back for winter, and you will find your surroundings more in keeping with the event commemorated by the granite pillar which now occupies the place where a very public gibbet used to stand.

It was here, on 8 November 1752, in the gathering dusk of a wet and stormy afternoon, that there was hanged James Stewart of Acharn, *Seumas a'Ghlinne*, James of the Glen; sentenced to death, said the authorities of the time, for his part in the murder of a public servant; 'executed on this spot,' reads the wording on his Ballachulish memorial, 'for a crime of which he was not guilty.'

James Stewart belonged to Duror. So do I. It was to this little community, some five or six miles to the south of Ballachulish on the road to Oban, that my Cameron grandparents moved in 1937 when my grandfather, having reached the age of 65, was obliged to relinquish his tied house on the Kingairloch estate where he had been employed since the start of the century.

It was in Duror that John and Catherine Cameron's daughter, Jean, my mother, met my father, Donald Hunter, whose own parents had then not been all that long in the place.

James Hunter, Donald's father, my grandfather and the man I was named after, had been born in 1880 at Cults in Aberdeenshire where his father and my great-grandfather, Cumming Hunter, an Ayrshire man, was then working as a gamekeeper.

On leaving school, James Hunter had followed his father into the keepering trade. This took him eventually to Coll in the Hebrides and, while living and working there, James married Flora MacPhail whose parents had a croft at Cornaigmore on the neighbouring island of Tiree.

She was a formidably clever and determined woman, my Tiree grandmother. There survives from 1899 an official document in which the Lords of the Privy Council for Education in Scotland confirm that Flora MacPhail, a scholar in Cornaigmore Public School, having shown proficiency in reading, writing, arithmetic and English, and having taken 'efficient instruction in an approved curriculum of studies embracing the subjects of geography and British history', had been awarded the Scottish Education Department's Merit Certificate.

This was sufficient to get the young Flora a teaching post at Acha in Coll where, of course, she met my grandfather. Their wedding – at a time when marriage was generally thought to bring to an end such limited career prospects as were then open to women – might have been expected to result in her giving up employment. But not only did my grandmother insist on continuing with her teaching, she remained anxious to pursue her own education and in 1924, at the age of 38, she obtained an honours degree in history from St Andrew's University.

It is hard to understand now how Flora Hunter managed this. Women graduates of any sort were few and far between in the 1920s. Women graduates from the Highlands and Islands were rarer still. Women graduates who had completed their studies while simultaneously holding down a job and having children were so exceptional as to have made my grandmother virtually unique.

Her degree was taken by correspondence. Her studying was necessarily combined with bringing up a steadily expanding family. And what is most astonishing of all is the fact that, in an era when motherhood was considered quite incompatible with the continuation of one's profession, Flora Hunter somehow succeeded in persuading Argyll County Council that she should be permitted to retain her successive teaching posts through several pregnancies. She taught until each baby was practically due. At her own expense, she hired a temporary replacement for a few weeks on either side of her six separate confinements. Then she was back into her classroom, back into the care of her own children, back into the running of a household. Her total workload – even without the added burden of her university course – was quite beyond our modern imagining.

The First World War separated James and Flora Hunter as it did most couples of their generation, my grandfather serving as a machine gunner with the Ayrshire Yeomanry on the Western Front, my grandmother being left to manage things single-handedly at home.

The family had now moved to the Argyll mainland, to the village of Portsonachan beside Loch Awe where my father was born. There he lived until my grandmother and grandfather moved, in 1928, to Duror: she to take charge of the local, single-teacher school; he to take a job as a trapper – what, in the more conservation-conscious climate of the 1990s is called a ranger – with the Forestry Commission which had begun establishing one of its earliest Highland plantations in Glen Duror some eight or nine years before.

One of my father's sisters, Mary, was to follow Flora Hunter as teacher in Duror Primary School. And my father himself, on his demobilisation at the end of the Second World War, by which time my grandfather had reached retirement age, was to become the Commission's second Hunter trapper in Glen Duror.

So my latest visit to the place to which James Stewart owed his Gaelic designation, *Seumas a'Ghlinne*, James of the Glen, is anything but a venture into unknown territory. The remains of James's house, standing in a more than usually extensive clearing in the spruce trees on the Beinn a'Bheithir flank of the valley, constituted one of the more familiar landmarks by which my father, when I used to accompany him on his treks in search of the deer whose numbers it was his business to keep firmly in check, measured our progress up or down Glen Duror. We regularly 'took our piece' – or, as might be said in a less Scottish brand of English, ate our sandwiches – in the shelter of the stone walls that had once been home to the man they hanged, on the other side of Beinn a'Bheithir, at Ballachulish.

The ten years which have passed since my last visit to the place have brought changes to Glen Duror. The black-painted stables which the Forestry Commission long ago built beside Seumas a'Ghlinne's former farmhouse – in order to provide accommodation for the horses which were still being used in the 1960s to carry out the timber-dragging functions nowadays performed by high-powered mechanical winches – have been converted into one of those overnight shelters which are maintained in several of Scotland's more remote locations by the Mountain Bothies Association. The battered notebook in which the MBA invites visitors to record their comments contains the usual celebrations of heroic climbs on the surrounding peaks and scarcely less heroic binges in the various pubs of Duror, Ballachulish and Glencoe. But one entry, I observe, was made by someone searching for the few surviving traces of James of the Glen. I make another entry to the same effect.

This particular November day is grey, cold and unusually still. The scarcely moving clouds are just concealing Sgurr Dhonuill and Sgurr Dhearg, the highest points on the long, horseshoe-shaped ridge of Beinn a'Bheithir. There is no sound of birdsong; only the noise made by the waters of the river at the foot of the slope where James Stewart once pastured his cows.

When sheep eventually took the place of cattle in Glen Duror, James's house came to be occupied by a shepherd. Later it was taken over by the Forestry Commission and its thatch replaced by corrugated iron. Now it has the increasingly tumbledown, nettle-surrounded look of so many of the abandoned dwellings which can be seen when exploring among the Highland hills.

Opposite James Stewart's former farm is the northern face of Fraochaidh. I still tend to think of that particular hill as virtually treeless, which is how it was when I was growing up. But Fraochaidh, which had previously been part of the Duror farm of Acharn, was bought by the Forestry Commission towards the end of the 1960s. And some twenty years ago, when employed by the commission for the two or three months of my summer vacation from university, I had helped the then head forester in Glen Duror – a man by the name of Lawrence Sinclair – to survey the line of the deer fence which was to mark the upper limit of planting on the Forestry Commission's latest acquisition.

Today Fraochaidh is thickly forested up to the 1,300-feet contour. But the older plantations on Beinn a'Bheithir's lower slopes have been very largely felled in the course of the last decade and hillsides which I always knew in their heavily wooded state now seem curiously naked and exposed. Walking down Glen Duror, and seeing landscape features which I had never seen before, it occurs to me that the place – which has, of course, been replanted with trees which are already several feet high – must look much the same as it did when my grandfather and namesake, James Hunter, first came here in the 1920s.

I was the third generation of my family to have collected a weekly pay packet from him, Lawrence Sinclair once remarked to me as I took my place in the queue which formed each Friday evening at the Forestry Commision office at Achindarroch, near the foot of Glen Duror.

There is no such queue today. When my father started work here at the end of Hitler's war he was one of nearly fifty employees for whom Lawrence Sinclair was responsible. Now, despite the fact that the Forestry Commission has massively expanded its Duror landholdings, its local workforce numbers barely half a dozen. The sawmill which was operated by my uncle, Jackie Cameron, has long since disappeared. So have most of the many Forestry Commission sheds and other buildings of my boyhood. Even Lawrence Sinclair's office, which I once thought to be as enduring as the man himself, has been demolished. Whatever benefits the forestry industry may currently be bringing to Duror and other Highland places like it, employment is most certainly not one of them.

Duror, which had formerly been part of the lands of the Lordship of the Isles, had belonged, for several centuries prior to the birth of James of the Glen in the years around 1700, to the Stewarts of Appin. Firmly Jacobite in their politics and just as firmly Episcopalian in their religion, the Stewarts had fought with Alasdair MacColla at Inverlochy. They were to turn out equally enthusiastically for Charles Edward Stuart in 1745 when some three hundred men from the various villages and hamlets strung out along the eastern shore of Loch Linnhe between Ballachulish and Creagan were to be among the troops who made that fateful and final Highland charge at the Battle of Culloden.

Not all these men – of whom no less than half were to be killed or wounded in that mad engagement – were actually called Stewart. Mostly they had names like Livingston, MacCombie, MacCorquodale, Carmichael and MacColl, names which, for all the population movements of the last two hundred years, can still be found here and there in Appin and in Duror. But their officers were Stewarts: the minor lairds and tacksmen of Achnacone, Achara, Invernahyle, Keil and Ballachulish taking their traditional place at the head of one or other of the Appin Regiment's eight companies, with Charles Stewart of Ardshiel assuming overall command.

In his native Gaelic Ardshiel was called *Tearlach Mor*, big Charles. A clearly formidable individual, he was the sort of man around whom legends grew. As a youth, it was said, Ardshiel had not only dared to cross swords with none other than Rob Roy MacGregor, that most renowned of Highland outlaws, but he had actually drawn MacGregor's blood. It was as a result of his undoubted fighting abilities, coupled with the fact that the Appin chieftaincy happened to be held in 1745 by a man who was both very young and totally unskilled in military matters, that Charles Stewart of Ardshiel had led the Appin men to war.

Charles Stewart escaped with his life at Culloden. But he was not to escape the other consequences of the Jacobite defeat – the repression and reprisals which the Hanoverian government now unleashed on the Highlands and Islands with a view to ensuring that the region's people would cause their southern rulers no further difficulty.

'I tremble for fear that this vile spot may still be the ruin of this island and our family,' King George's son and Britain's newest hero, the Duke of Cumberland, is said to have remarked of northern Scotland following his victory. He need not have worried. There was among his own troops no lack of individuals determined to ensure that the Highlands and Islands, as the leading London politician, the Duke of Newcastle, had so plainly put it, be 'absolutely reduced'.

A good start had been made with burnings and destruction of the type already undertaken by the Royal Navy in Morvern. Now, as the spring of 1746 began to turn into summer, Cumberland's redcoated soldiers followed enthusiastically where the sailors and marines had led. His troops had been 'dispersed through the several parts of this heathenish country', one officer wrote from the Great Glen towards the end of May. Homes were being burned. Goods were being seized. Cattle were being taken. 'We take care,' it was reported of the army's treatment of the Highland population, 'to leave them with no sustenance.'

To Ardshiel there came the particularly brutal and unpleasant Captain Caroline Scott who, throughout the Jacobite rebellion, had successfully held the army outpost of Fort William in the face of a determined Cameron siege.

While Charles Stewart, in order to avoid the hanging that Scott had already meted out to several of his captives, hid from successive military patrols in a cave which can still be seen behind a waterfall on a hill burn above Lagnaha Farm in Duror, his fine house on the shore of Loch Linnhe opposite Ardgour was systematically destroyed. The slates were taken from its roof. Its internal timbers were removed. Its walls were dismantled stone by stone. And on the Stewart laird's wife having the temerity to ask what was now to happen to her and her children, Scott roughly presented the homeless woman with a boll of her own oatmeal and told her to look for help from those of her relatives who were still to be found in Appin or in Duror.

One of these relatives was Seumas a'Ghlinne, Charles Stewart's illegitimate half-brother and the man whom Ardshiel, who finally made his escape to France in September 1746, appointed to take charge of his affairs. James, too, had fought at Culloden. But his part in Prince Charles Edward's rebellion had been more modest than that of his Ardshiel kinsman and there was no immediate risk of his being seized on the treason charges which were then being so energetically preferred against more prominent Highland Jacobites.

When Ardshiel's lands were expropriated by the government and placed in the hands of the commissioners who had been appointed to administer all such 'forfeited estates' on behalf of the Crown, however, James was obliged – as a result of a ruling which made it impossible for the Forfeited Estates Commissioners to lease land to the relations of any Jacobite fugitive, such as Charles Stewart, who was still at large – to give up his farm in Glen Duror and to take another tack, or tenancy, at Acharn. But he was otherwise unmolested.

While continuing to keep in close contact with the exiled Charles Stewart, on whose behalf he collected an entirely unofficial and ostensibly secret 'rent' from families living on the Ardshiel estate, James developed friendly enough relations with Colin Campbell of Glenure – the man whom the government had taken on as factor, or manager, of Ardshiel's confiscated possessions. His principal objective, James Stewart seems to have concluded, pragmatically and sensibly enough, ought to consist of doing what he could to make things as secure as possible both for Ardshiel's family and his tenantry.

Problems eventually cropped up, however; these problems centring on a number of tenants whom Colin Campbell decided – for no better reason perhaps than to demonstrate his anti-Jacobite zeal to his superiors in Edinburgh – to evict from their holdings at Achindarroch. These tenants – three Mac-Combies, a MacCorquodale and a MacColl – were closely acquainted with James Stewart. Their various little bits of ground were within half a mile of James's new home at Acharn. It was inevitable, therefore, that the Achindarroch people should come to James Stewart for assistance. Not only was he more skilled than themselves in the ways of the wider world, but he was fluent, unlike most of his neighbours, in the English needed to make their case to the authorities.

This Seumas a'Ghlinne, as he was still known, proceeded energetically to do; making no small nuisance of himself in the process; engaging lawyers; travelling to Edinburgh in order to badger various officials; getting himself on increasingly bad terms with Colin Campbell. When the latter was killed on 15 May 1752, therefore, it was virtually inevitable that some part of the suspicion should immediately fall on James Stewart – the more so since the factor's assassination occurred just prior to the date fixed for the now highly contentious evictions at Achindarroch.

On the day of his death, Campbell of Glenure was returning from business in Lochaber. Accompanied by three colleagues, he had been ferried across the then bridgeless narrows at Ballachulish in late afternoon and had immediately ridden southward towards Kentallen and Duror on a track a good deal higher than the modern road which here sticks closely to the shoreline. A mile or so from the ferry, at a spot marked still by a cairn now surrounded by yet another Forestry Commission plantation, the party was startled by the sound of a single shot. Campbell, mortally wounded, fell headlong from his horse and, as his companions rushed to his aid, a man was glimpsed among the birch trees on the hillside above.

This particular individual, the authorities rapidly concluded, was Allan Stewart or *Ailean Breac* – a rootless and restless young man who, among other equally dubious accomplishments, had managed to see action on both sides in the course of the 1745 rebellion. Allan, whose Gaelic nickname *Breac* derived from the fact that his face had been pitted and marked by a severe attack of smallpox, had decided early on a career in soldiering and had consequently joined an English infantry detachment prior to Prince Charles Edward Stuart's arrival in Scotland. Captured by the Jacobites in the course of the Battle of Prestonpans, he had promptly enlisted with the Appin Regiment – among whose officers, of course, was Seumas a'Ghlinne in whose Glen Duror home the parentless Allan had spent much of his childhood.

Having helped Charles Stewart of Ardshiel evade Cumberland's dragoons in the weeks following the Culloden débâcle, Allan had finally followed his patron to Paris where – as keen as ever on the military life – he enlisted in the French army.

But for all that the British authorities were anxious to have him hanged as a deserter, a rebel and a traitor, Allan was known to have been revisiting Duror and, more specifically, James Stewart's farm of Acharn in the spring of 1752. He had been heard to make characteristically violent and vainglorious statements as to his ability to sort out Colin Campbell of Glenure. And the figure seen so briefly by the latter's colleagues at the moment of the factor's death conformed – or could be readily made to conform – to Allan Stewart's description.

Allan was immediately and formally accused of Colin Campbell's murder. But Allan, despite the best efforts of the soldiers who were soon combing every

IAIN ANDERSON, STRATHAIRD, ISLE OF SKYE

glen and pass between Duror and the east coast ports, was nowhere to be found. It was consequently necessary for Scotland's rulers – who were determined that Glenure's assassination should be speedily and spectacularly avenged – to cast their net a little wider.

On the evening following the death of the factor, a platoon of redcoated troops from the army garrison at Fort William came to the dramhouse at Inshaig in Duror. There they arrested James Stewart of Acharn and charged him with complicity in the killing of Colin Campbell.

That September James appeared in court in Inveraray. He was a Stewart and a Jacobite on trial for his supposed part in the murder of a Campbell and a Hanoverian in the place that was both Clan Campbell's capital and a major centre of Hanoverian power. On the bench sat Scotland's Lord Justice General, Archibald Campbell, Duke of Argyll. Among the fifteen jurymen were no fewer than eleven other members of the Campbell gentry. Irrespective of the quality of the evidence against him – evidence that was both weak and circumstantial – it would have been miraculous, in such politically weighted circumstances, if James Stewart had been found anything other than guilty. There were no miracles – not then, not subsequently.

They took him under heavily armed escort from his Fort William cell to Ballachulish on a day so wild that it proved impossible for several hours to cross on the ferry. They hanged him in the wind and rain. They chained his corpse to an iron-clad gibbet. They posted a guard of fifteen soldiers to prevent his body being cut down by friends and sympathisers. As a singularly dramatic warning to all the British government's actual and potential opponents in the Highlands, James Stewart was to swing there on that hillock above Ballachulish Ferry: not for hours, nor days, nor months, but years.

Slowly his flesh rotted. Slowly his bones were cleaned and bleached by sun and storm. At last, more than two years after his execution, James Stewart's skeleton was blown to the ground. But the ever-present representatives of the much vaunted civilisation which Britain's rulers then proclaimed themselves to be bringing to this part of Scotland were there to wire the bones together and string them up a second time.

More months passed. The wire rusted. The bones fell earthwards one by one. Gradually they were collected by Stewart of Ballachulish whose home was no more than quarter of a mile away and whose small daughter would long afterwards recall how she had carefully washed James Stewart's skull with her own hands. Eventually, when the patient and painstaking Stewart laird of Ballachulish had gathered every earthly fragment of his kinsman into his possession, he took Seumas a'Ghlinne back to Duror, burying him in the ancient church at Keil, one of the many places of worship in this part of the West Highlands which has long been thought to have been founded by none other than Columba.

Driving north from Keil on another November afternoon nearly two-and-a-half centuries after James Stewart's death, I call at Innes MacColl's shop and post office. I grew up in the immediately adjacent house and it was from Innes's father, Angus, that I first heard something of the many tales and stories surrounding Seumas a'Ghlinne, whose then ruinous and now largely demolished house at Acharn was one of the spots where I played often as a boy.

Innes MacColl's family is now the only one in Duror to have roots that stretch back to James Stewart's time. One of the Duror shopkeeper's female ancestors is reputed to have been the person made responsible by James's father for the care of the illegitimate child who would one day be seized at Inshaig – no more than a couple of hundred yards from the spot where Innes and I are talking.

We are speaking, as we do in the course of all our occasional encounters, of the extent to which Duror has altered in recent decades; of the fact that there is scarcely a person in the district with whom either of us went to school; of how there is now nobody hereabouts from whom it is possible to hear Duror tradition of the sort so familiar to Innes's father and to others of his generation.

From Innes I buy a copy of this week's *Oban Times*. 'Duror Furore', reads the headline over a story about the campaign which has been mounted locally in an attempt to prevent the construction of several new houses in the part of Duror called Cuil Bay. The planned development, say the objectors, would 'spoil' Duror. Perhaps it would. But I doubt if the many MacColls and Livingstons and others now keeping James Stewart company in the old graveyard at Keil would feel that there is a great deal of their Duror left today to spoil.

The forces which were thus to strip so many of our Scottish Highland communities of their people were all too evident at the Inveraray trial of Seumas a'Ghlinne; evident, above all, in the person of the most fervent of the prosecution lawyers, Simon Fraser.

Fraser's father was the Lord Lovat beheaded by the British government for his part in the proceedings which culminated at Culloden. The son, too, may have participated in the battle; the facts are unclear. What is all too apparent, however, is the rapidity with which the young man concluded that if he was to regain his family's lands, to say nothing of its titles and its influence, the most prudent course to adopt was one that demonstrated his unswerving devotion to that self-same political establishment which had so ruthlessly executed his own father. Hence the zeal with which Simon harried James Stewart in the Inveraray courtroom; and hence the equal zeal which he was soon displaying in raising Highland regiments to fight in Britain's foreign wars.

The French forces which were overwhelmed by the British at Quebec in 1759 included Jacobite fugitives from Scotland. But they were massively outnumbered by those Highlanders now serving under Hanoverian colours. And it was not with the Jacobites but with the unctuously loyalist Simon Fraser and the various other individuals responsible for having so successfully put Highland military prowess at the disposal of the imperial authorities that the future of the northern part of Scotland very obviously lay. More comprehensively than could ever have been envisaged by the men who had framed the Statutes of Iona, the Gaelic aristocracy of the Scottish Highlands had begun to turn their backs forever on their past.

Men of Ruairi Mor MacLeod's stamp were no longer in charge at Dunvegan. Nor were they to be found in any of the other former centres of clan power. Castle halls which had once resounded with music were now without mirth, without merriment, without pleasure, without the passing round of drinking horns, without feasting, without liberality to men of learning, without as much as a single voice raised tunefully in song. So said one island bard before the seventeenth century had ended. So others were to comment bitterly before many years had passed. These trends had been evident long before Prince Charles Edward Stuart landed in Scotland. But they were massively reinforced and accelerated as a result both of the crushing of his rising and the consequent determination of the British government to obliterate as many as possible of those features which had previously made the Scottish Highlands so different from other parts of the country.

Episcopalian clerics were expelled from their pulpits and replaced with Presbyterians. Highlanders were forbidden to carry weapons. The traditional tartan plaid was banned. The Gaelic language was further marginalised. Clan chiefs were stripped of much of their traditional authority and strongly encouraged to model themselves rather less on their warrior ancestors and rather more on the commercially minded nobility who now held sway politically in England and the Scottish Lowlands.

This latter transformation was to be astonishingly complete. Although there were no descendants of those Stewart gentry who had fought at Culloden still living permanently in Duror when I was a boy, more than one Stewart family was in the habit of returning to the place each summer. But so removed were these holidaymakers, in both their manner and their outlook, from the rest of us that, as children, we thought the visiting Stewarts to be English. And if someone had put it to us – which nobody ever did – that the Duror Stewarts had once spoken the Argyll Gaelic which we still heard occasionally from our own grandparents, we would have considered such a suggestion to be patently absurd.

Men increasingly accustomed, as the former chieftains of the Scottish Highlands had become within a very few years of Culloden, to mingling with the monied southern aristocrats who then dominated the Edinburgh and London social scene were unavoidably obliged to adopt a set of values very different from those which had been held by the likes of Ruairi Mor. 'The number and bravery of their followers no longer supports their grandeur,' it was commented at the time. 'The number and weight of their guineas only are put in the scale.'

Having seen at first hand something of the impact of this very fundamental shift in attitudes, that most incisive Englishman, Dr Samuel Johnson, whose trip to the Scottish Highlands in 1773 made him one of the region's earliest tourists, drew a highly prescient conclusion.

'There was perhaps never any change of national manners,' wrote Johnson, 'so quick, so great and so general as that which has operated in the Highlands by the late conquest and the subsequent laws .... The clans retain little now of their original character. Their ferocity of temper is softened, their military ardour is extinguished, their dignity of independence is depressed, their contempt for government subdued and their reverence for their chiefs abated.'

Where once there had been 'patriarchal rulers', the visiting Englishman observed gloomily, there were now 'rapacious landlords'; men who had 'no more hesitation' than their counterparts elsewhere, as another equally perceptive – if slightly more circumspect – observer put it, 'in turning their estates to the best advantage'.

In the course of one of his many skirmishes with the occupying force which Oliver Cromwell despatched to Lochaber, a seventeenth-century Cameron of Locheil, in a gesture which would have done justice to a Gaelic saga hero of a thousand years earlier, had bitten out the throat of the English officer who had pinned him to the ground. That man's eighteenth-century descendants, however, were soon so intimately embroiled with the forces their predecessor had been so spectacularly resisting as to be selling their ancient woodlands to southern iron smelters and, with the capital thus realised, investing in the highly lucrative West Indies trade.

GREY DAY IN STEWART COUNTRY

Nor were other chiefs-cum-landlords any less willing to break with what had gone before. All sorts of reverberations inevitably resulted. The Highland aristocracy's new and lavish lifestyles – a constant heartbreak to those Gaelic poets who endlessly lamented the extent to which fine clothes, imported furnishings and other fripperies now loomed so large in the calculations of their former patrons – cost a great deal of money. The consequent quest for ever-larger incomes resulted, in turn, in the practically universal adoption of estate management methods which, because they placed much more emphasis on the proprietor's need for cash than they did on the ancient responsibilities of kinship, were as socially disruptive as they were economically novel.

When, in 1739, MacLeod of Dunvegan and MacDonald of Sleat tried to sell Skye people to American plantation owners, the two aspiring entrepreneurs effectively gave notice that the age-old obligations owed by chiefs to their clans were now to be wholly disregarded by men increasingly inclined to view their tenantries as exploitable resources rather than as fellow human beings with whom they were indissolubly connected by both blood and custom.

The generous, open-handed chiefs of former days had gone, declared a

Hebridean poet of the 1760s; those great men 'who had regard for their faithful followers' were, alas, no more. 'Look around you,' that bard urged the ever more impoverished Gaels, 'and see the nobility without pity for poor folk, without kindness to friends. They are of the opinion that you do not belong to the soil and though they have left you destitute they cannot see it as a loss.'

Seumas a'Ghlinne had died because he had chosen to make a stand on behalf of tenants facing imminent evictions. Many others of James Stewart's class – those tacksmen or more prominent tenants who had come to constitute a Gaelic-speaking gentry and who had provided successive Highland armies with their officer corps – left Scotland rather than be party to the cruelties which now became commonplace. 'Families who had not been disturbed for four or five hundred years are turned out of house and home and their possessions given to the highest bidder,' wrote the understandably embittered emigrant son of one such Cameron tacksman from Lochaber. 'So much for Highland attachment between chief and clan.'

That was in 1804 when Cameron of Locheil and every other landlord in the north of Scotland was beginning to wake up to the fact that, though there was still money to be made from the cattle trade which had expanded so massively in the half-century following Culloden, there was much more money to be made from sheep-farming. This new form of agricultural production, however, could not be combined with the retention of a substantial human population. The introduction of sheep to the Highlands and Islands was consequently to involve evictions and expulsions on a scale which would have seemed quite inconceivable to men of the generation to which James Stewart of Acharn belonged.

From Duror I drive north through glens left largely empty by nineteenth-century clearances; through Glen Shiel, through Glen Carron and Strath Bran; through Easter Ross where, in 1792, several hundred men mustered in a vain attempt to expel both sheep and shepherds from this part of Scotland; on into Sutherland at Bonar Bridge where, in 1887, following the altogether more successful uprising mastermined by the Highland Land League, crofters presented Michael Davitt with the tribute I had seen exhibited in County Mayo.

This is now one of Europe's most thinly populated places; a locality which, with the onset of cold weather and the departure of the last of the season's tourists, is more bereft of people than virtually any other corner of our continent.

Some miles beyond Lairg, at a point where the road attains an altitude of several hundred feet, I stop in a roadside lay-by. The Atlantic Ocean is thirty miles to the west, the North Sea nearly forty miles to the east. The map tells me that, from this spot in the heart of Sutherland, I could readily walk these distances, supposing the terrain made such a journey feasible, without encountering a single human habitation.

Although it is barely a week into November, it snowed in the night and the otherwise brown moorland is still spattered with greyish patches of half-melted slush. The higher hills to the west are a much purer shade of white, the pools and lochans in the foreground a deep blue. The breeze from the north-west has a decidedly chill edge to it and the sky, in this brief gap between repeated squalls of sleet and hail, has taken on that curiously translucent quality found in the Scottish Highlands in winter when the wind is blowing, as it is today, straight off the Arctic ice.

In the more sheltered spots on the north shore of Loch Naver there are still some withered leaves clinging to the birches. But the sky has darkened. There are foam-streaked waves on the water. Soon it is snowing heavily; and snow is still falling when, travelling slowly down Strathnaver, I pause at Syre to inspect the square, stone house once occupied by Patrick Sellar.

When Sellar bought the Morvern estate on which my Dempster great-grandfather was eventually employed, he was a monied man well on in years. When he came first from his native Morayshire to this part of Sutherland towards the end of the nineteenth century's first decade, however, Sellar was a young, brash, pushy, overwhelmingly self-confident adventurer; every bit as convinced as any of the very similar personalities who were to be found at the empire's cutting edge in Africa that, for all the extreme measures which its pursuit might require on occasion, the securing and enhancement of individual wealth was both a necessary and a praiseworthy means of promoting Britain's interests in those localities which had not yet been brought fully within the ambit of the country's increasingly commercial civilisation.

For the people who had occupied Strathnaver for so many generations prior to his arrival, Patrick Sellar had only a profound and withering contempt. The Sutherland 'aborigines', as he habitually called them, were characterised in his opinion mainly by their 'sloth, poverty and filth'. They were a 'parcel of beggars' whose 'obstinate adherence' to Gaelic – a 'barbarous jargon' Sellar called it – had wholly isolated them from 'the enlightened nations of Europe' and left them in that 'state of society' which one might expect to encounter among 'savages'.

Just like their tribal counterparts in other parts of the world, however, the Strathnaver folk – for all their alleged backwardness – possessed lands which men of Sellar's stamp thought well worth obtaining. This long, wide valley running northwards to the sea, reported a professional land agent in 1810 was

SUNRISE, AIRIGH MHUILLIN, SOUTH UIST

SUN SETTING OVER UIST

DUNADD, ARGYLL

MACHAIR, IONA

LONBAIN, THE APPLECROSS PENINSULA

GLEN SHIEL

THE LOCHABER HILLS FROM HIGHBRIDGE

THE SOUTH FORD BETWEEN BENBECULA AND SOUTH UIST AT DUSK

LOOKING SOUTH FROM BENBECULA TO THE SOUTH UIST HILLS

RUINED COTTAGE, STRONTIAN

MOVING CATTLE IN GLEANN GEAL, MORVERN

FISHING OFF THE OLD PIER, CREAGORRY, BENBECULA

'a very pleasing and agreeable' locality; a place habitually producing 'good and early' crops of grain. Patrick Sellar, having quickly gained a position of some influence with the strath's owners, the Countess of Sutherland and her recently acquired English husband, the Marquis of Stafford, accordingly determined to have Strathnaver for himself.

In the bitterly cold weather which enveloped Sutherland towards the close of 1813, the necessary legal papers were issued to the scores of families then living in the strath. The following spring these same families were evicted to make way for Patrick Sellar's Cheviot sheep and their Borders shepherds. Some at least of the Strathnaver houses were burned or otherwise destroyed by the evictors, as was the common practice of the time in the Highlands, in order to ensure that those dwellings which had been cleared of their inhabitants could not subsequently be reoccupied.

Angus MacKay, then a boy of eleven, long afterwards told a royal commission of enquiry something of the quite horrific human circumstances surrounding those events.

His father, mother and elder brother had left their Strathnaver home with the family's livestock at first light on the day scheduled for their removal, Angus MacKay explained, their township having 'got notice' that a financial penalty would be imposed on anyone found to be keeping animals on any part of Patrick Sellar's newly created, and enormously extensive, sheep farm.

'They rose in the morning and went away with the cattle, a horse, two mares and two foals to the place they were to live in after, and left me and my brothers, who were younger, sleeping in the bed.'

While it was still early, said Angus MacKay, a woman from a neighbouring family arrived to tell the boys to rouse themselves because Sellar had begun destroying houses in an adjacent township.

'We got such a fright that we started out of bed and ran down to the river, because there was a friend of ours living upon the other side and we wished to go there for protection. I took my brother on my back and through the river I went.'

But the water was deep and fast-flowing and the smaller of the boys, feeling it rise over his body, quite naturally panicked. 'My brother commenced shaking,' remembered Angus MacKay, 'and I fell and he gripped around my neck and I could not rise or move.'

Both lads were sobbing now in their terror, convinced that they were about to drown. Fortunately for them, however, 'there was a woman coming up the strath and she saw us and jumped into the river and swept us out of it.'

Angus MacKay regarded the members of the government enquiry team who had asked him to appear before them – the MPs, the landlords, the various men of substance whom Prime Minister William Gladstone had instructed to look into the crofting population's many grievances.

'It would be a very hard heart but would mourn to see the the circumstances of the people that day,' he pronounced. 'He would be a very cruel man who would not mourn for the people.'

In the Strathnaver of his boyhood, Angus MacKay affirmed, there had been innumerable settlements – 'touns' he called them in the manner of the Lowland Scots with whom he had no doubt become acquainted in the course of his long life. 'If you were going up the strath now,' he told the royal commission, 'you would see on both sides of it the places where the touns were. You would see a mile or half a mile between each toun. There were four or five families in each of these touns and bonnie haughs between the touns …. The people had plenty of flocks of goats, sheep, horses and cattle, and they were living happy.'

There was much noise and turmoil in Strathnaver in May 1814. 'For some days after the people were turned out,' Mr Gladstone's royal commission were informed by another of their more elderly Sutherland witnesses, 'one could scarcely hear a word with the lowing of cattle and the screaming of children marching off in all directions.'

Then there was quiet. 'All was silence and desolation', runs one contemporary description of the immediate aftermath of a Sutherland clearance of the Strathnaver type. 'Blackened and roofless huts still enveloped in smoke, articles of furniture cast away as of no value to the houseless, and a few domestic fowl scraping for food among the hills of ashes were the only objects that told us of man. A few days had sufficed to change a countryside, teeming with the cheeriest sounds of rural life, into a desert.' Strathnaver is a desert still.

In the slanting afternoon sunshine which has followed the earlier shower of snow, I inspect the remnants of Rossal, just one among the many 'touns' to which Angus MacKay directed that royal commission more than a hundred years ago. The foundations of several homes, together with the outlines of their immediately adjacent byres or cowsheds, can still be clearly seen; and I recall how an archaeologist who excavated the Rossal ruins in the 1960s told me how, when digging in one of those byres, he could smell cowdung which had somehow been preserved there, far below the turf, since the morning when Patrick Sellar's men had removed the building's roof.

It was one of Sellar's standard justifications for what he was about that the families he was evicting were both impoverished and starving. They would certainly not have attained to what we reckon comfort. But the sheer size of their houses – larger by far than the one in which my own grandfather spent his Strontian boyhood and much more spacious, for that matter, than the Glasgow tenement rooms in which not a few of Strathnaver's dispossessed would end their days – are indicative of living standards not too dismal by comparison with those which then prevailed elsewhere.

The township's surroundings tell the same story. Rossal's undulating, grassy fields, on which a flock of North Country Cheviot sheep are grazing, have the fertile and productive appearance of good land. Its agricultural attractiveness, after all, was what caused Patrick Sellar so to covet this locality.

'The aborigines, the common people, are effectively cowed,' the sheep-farmer informed one of the Marquis of Stafford's representatives when the Strathnaver clearances were at an end. And though both the Marquis and his lady, that latest representative of a family to which successive generations of Sutherland folk had given unstinting allegiance, were beginning to be the recipients of some adverse comment in the south, Patrick Sellar had no hesitation in attributing the highest possible motives to the man and woman in whose name an entire population had been forcibly transferred from inland

ANDREW MACCOLL, LOBSTER FISHERMAN, SCOURIE, SUTHERLAND

places like Strathnaver and afterwards resettled in distant coastal locations where, though they were provided with crofts or lotts, care was taken to ensure that these newly laid out holdings were so diminutive as to oblige their recipients to involve themselves in the fishing industry for which Sutherland's owners entertained high hopes.

'Lord and Lady Stafford,' Sellar wrote in 1815, 'were pleased humanely to order a new arrangement of this country. That the interior should be possessed by cheviot shepherds and the people brought down to the coast and placed there in lotts under the size of three arable acres, sufficient for the maintenance of an industrious family, but pinched enough to cause them to turn their attention to the fishing. I presume to say that the proprietors humanely ordered this arrangement, because it surely was a most benevolent action to put these barbarous hordes into a position where they could better associate together, apply to industry, educate their children and advance in civilisation.'

The Strathnaver people, the wider world was informed by the Sutherland estate management's most senior representative, the lawyer and MP, James Loch, 'settled into their new lotts at Strathy with the utmost cheerfulness'. When finally provided with an opportunity to make public his own recollection of this particular migration, however, Angus MacKay gave a very different account of it.

'Strathy Point is two miles in length on one side and three upon the other,' he said. 'The westerly wind blows upon it, the north-west wind blows upon it, the north-east wind blows upon it.' So exposed was the place that little could be made of its small crofts. As to fishing, this was no place to be launching a boat.

Taking the road that the Strathnaver refugee column would have followed with its livestock and its more portable belongings, I reach Strathy Point just as the sun is setting. Westward the rugged Sutherland coast stretches away towards Cape Wrath. Eastward and north-eastward are the hills of Orkney and the high cliffs of Dunnet Head in Caithness. Travel due north from Strathy Point and no land would be encountered on this side of the pole.

Here there are none of Strathnaver's wide fields, nothing of that natural shelter which ensured that, prior to my leaving Rossal, the breeze had dropped away completely. At Strathy Point, projecting abruptly into some of the stormiest seas in the world, the wind is blowing strongly. The waves are breaking whitely on dark rocks. To have been removed here from a place like Rossal must, indeed, have been heartbreaking.

At Bettyhill I call on John Kenneth MacKay, a crofter and a former postman whom I got to know when he became the chairman of the local branch of the Scottish Crofters Union. We talk about Strathnaver – to which his own people once belonged – and what it must have meant to be transported down here to the infinitely less attractive plots of land on which crofters like John Kenneth are still living.

'It might seem nice enough here now on a good day,' John Kenneth says. 'But just you take a look at the stone dykes around the fields, the heaps of stones you still see scattered here and there. Every single one of these rocks had to be shifted by hand by the folk who were settled here at the beginning of last century.'

We sit in silence for a while. 'I don't feel bitter about it,' John Kenneth comments. 'There is no point in bitterness. But the clearance of Strathnaver should never be forgotten.'

It was John Kenneth MacKay who built the monument which now stands beside the modern Strathnaver road just across the river from Rossal. It

JOHN KENNETH MACKAY OF BETTYHILL, SUTHERLAND

165

commemorates both that community's destruction and the desperate efforts made by a Rossal stonemason, Donald MacLeod, to obtain justice for his people.

A propagandist and a pamphleteer of genius, MacLeod became a merciless critic of the Sutherland estate, its owners and its agents. But it is indicative of the quite overwhelming strength of the forces ranged against both this Rossal man and Scottish Highlanders generally that, while the penniless Donald MacLeod was forced eventually to emigrate to Canada, his leading adversaries, Patrick Sellar and the Marquis of Stafford, went on to add still further to their power and privileges – the marquis becoming a duke and his principal sheep-farming tenant acquiring, at Ardtornish, his own Highland estate.

In 1816, thanks to the persistence of a Gaelic-speaking sheriff whose sympathies, most unusually for that time, lay with the Highland people rather than their landlords, Sellar was tried at Inverness on charges arising from the cruelties he was alleged to have inflicted on some of the several hundred families evicted from Strathnaver in May 1814. At stake in that Inverness courtroom was more than Patrick Sellar's reputation. What was at issue was the entire policy of clearance; a policy in which there was invested the reputation of some of the most influential men in Scotland.

The judge spoke eloquently of what he described as the 'humanity of disposition' shown by the accused. In the jury box sat eight landed proprietors, four of Sellar's fellow agriculturalists, two Highland businessmen and a lawyer. It was as likely, in such circumstances, that the Strathnaver sheep farmer would be found guilty as it had been probable, some sixty years earlier in Inveraray, that James Stewart would be declared innocent. Patrick Sellar accordingly went free.

Nearly two centuries later, I stand in the early evening darkness at John Kenneth MacKay's memorial to Donald MacLeod and I look across to Rossal. I had seen both red deer and sheep in the headlights of my car as I came slowly up the strath. But here there is no sign of any kind of life. The Milky Way arches dimly overhead. The frost-stiffened grass crunches softly under my boots. The River Naver, where two small boys so nearly drowned on the morning of Patrick Sellar's clearance, runs loudly in the cold, still night.

There is, perhaps, some sense of satisfaction to be got from being able, in our arguably overcrowded country, thus to escape completely from the omnipresent impact of humanity. But Strathnaver does not seem to me to be a temple to wild nature. It seems rather to encapsulate the consequences of man's eternal inhumanity to man. I should prefer there still to be some lights each night in Rossal.

CHAPTER NINE

In Strathnaver I stayed with Donald and Morag MacLeod and their family. Morag manages the local post office. Donald, who is one of the Scottish Crofters Union's leading activists, combines his crofting with the part-time secretaryship of a very energetic community group, the North West Sutherland Council of Social Service. Both Donald and Morag are among the growing number of Highlanders who, despite their having obtained educational qualifications of the kind which used to result in the outward movement of so many younger people, are now committed to making a go of life in their own place. This is not always easy.

Crofts began by being small. Mostly they are small still. Few crofters, therefore, can earn an adequate livelihood simply by working their land. Other sources of income are required. And while new employment opportunities have become available in many parts of the Highlands and Islands in recent years, Strathnaver has not so far benefited greatly from them.

That there are still crofters in Strathnaver at all, of course, represents one small and belated Highland victory over Patrick Sellar. Donald MacLeod's people were among those who returned to one of Sellar's former farms in the early part of the present century when the British government – in response to the various campaigns mounted by the Highland Land League and its successor organisations – eventually established an official agency whose remit it was to purchase a number of depopulated Highland estates in order to resettle them with crofters.

From Donald's late father I heard some years ago how one of the families who came back to Strathnaver at that time included an old woman who, as a very small child, had been one of the victims of Patrick Sellar's clearance. This elderly lady's return to her birthplace, I think, is a powerful symbol. That she had survived to reclaim lands which had once seemed lost forever is indicative of the fact that, for all the hardships inflicted on so many Gaels by men of Sellar's type, the removal of Scottish Highlanders from their own place was neither final nor irrevocable. But on the raw, wet, windy night that has brought me to the Western Isles – and, more specifically, to South Uist – it is difficult to avoid the thought that, over most of the last two hundred years, setback and reversal have been altogether more commonplace than progress.

Here, following the collapse of the Lordship of the Isles, there came those foremost Gaelic bards, the MacMhuirichs. And half a century after the battle of Culloden there was still a Lachlan MacMhuirich living here. But what distinguished this MacMhuirich of the 1790s from the eighteen prior bearers of his name, what differentiated him so tragically from every one of the generations linking him to the thirteenth century and Irish-born progenitor of this extraordinarily learned family, was the fact that Lachlan MacMhuirich could neither read nor write his people's script. So complete now was the disintegration of Gaelic Scotland's civilisation that this man, whose predecessors had successively undergone so rigorous a training in Ireland's bardic schools, was personally quite unlettered. With his own eyes, he told enquirers after the literary treasures he was understandably – but erroneously – thought to have in his possession, he had seen the ancient manuscripts so long safeguarded by his kindred cut up and used to make a tailor's patterns.

Between the MacMhuirichs and those who had formerly been their sponsors there had ceased to be any meaningful connection. Ranald George MacDonald, twentieth chief of Clanranald, was one of the many Highlands and Islands aristocrats who, as the nineteenth century began, was much less interested in the maintenance of Gaelic tradition than he was in cutting something of a dash in London's high society.

Where Sutherland's proprietors looked to sheep and fishing to boost their revenues, Clanranald looked to kelp – an industrial alkali which was manufactured primarily from Hebridean seaweed and which was in great demand in the years around 1800. Clanranald's estates here in Benbecula and South Uist were accordingly divided into smallholdings of the same diminutive dimensions as those to which the Strathnaver people were consigned by Patrick Sellar. In the Uist case, however, the families who became the tenants of these new crofts were not ordered, as their Sutherland counterparts had been, to engage in fishing; rather they were compelled to produce the kelp on which Clanranald was soon depending for the bulk of what had become his quite enormous annual income.

But none of the substantial revenues thus generated were invested in developmental projects of a worthwhile sort. Instead, as one contemporary observer put it, they were 'bartered for the merest baubles' – being spent almost entirely on 'residences, dress, furniture, equipages' and the like – with the unavoidable result, when changes in southern manufacturing techniques brought the kelp boom to an end, that Clanranald, who had long forsaken Scotland for the south of England, went spectacularly bankrupt.

Benbecula and South Uist – together with the nearby island of Barra where another leading family, the MacNeils, had run into very similar financial difficulties – were now sold to Colonel John Gordon, an Aberdeenshire laird and businessman. Gordon was reputed to be Scotland's richest individual. His Uist and Barra tenants were among the country's most impoverished people. Having been deprived of such modest wages as they had earlier earned from their kelping activities, Gordon's crofters, like most of the rest of the Highlands and Islands population of the time, had become almost wholly reliant for their sustenance on potatoes – these being the one crop which a typically tiny croft could grow in sufficient quantity to come anywhere near providing the nutritional requirements of its occupying family.

In the 1840s, when potato blight first became endemic in Western Europe and when this vital crofting harvest was totally destroyed, Uist and Barra people simply starved.

The Church of Scotland minister, Norman MacLeod, yet another member of the far-flung clerical dynasty stemming from the manse of Morvern, came here in 1847, taking much the same route through Benbecula and South Uist as I have myself followed this dark and starless winter's evening.

'The scene of wretchedness which we witnessed as we entered on the estate of Colonel Gordon,' MacLeod reported, 'was deplorable, nay heart-rending. On the beach the whole population of the country seemed to be met, gathering the precious cockles … I never witnessed such countenances – starvation on many faces – the children with their melancholy looks, big-looking knees, shrivelled legs, hollow eyes, swollen-like bellies. God help them, I never did witness such wretchedness.'

There were those naïve enough to think that John Gordon might devote some part of his large fortune to the famine relief which was so manifestly needed on his Hebridean properties. But Gordon's preferred solution to these difficulties was altogether more direct. He proposed to rid his island estates of the vast bulk of their crofting tenants – those tenants constituting a population which John Gordon and his fellow landlords had generally taken to describing as 'redundant'.

The programme of evictions which had commenced in the time of Clanranald and MacNeil was now dramatically stepped up. Thousands of people were compulsorily removed from their crofts. Many were transported to Canada. Others were left to make their way to Lowland cities. From Glasgow and Edinburgh came newspaper reports of obviously famished, sick and ragged refugees from Barra, South Uist and Benbecula squatting hopelessly in the streets. From the other side of the Atlantic, meanwhile, there emanated a whole series of official despatches which were equally condemnatory of John Gordon's policy.

In all his 'long experience', wrote the resident medical supervisor at the Grosse Isle quarantine station in Canada's St Lawrence River, he had never seen a 'body of emigrants' who were 'so destitute of clothing and bedding' as the people disembarking from the disease-ridden ships which Gordon had chartered to carry his unwanted tenants to Britain's colonies in North America.

To be hungry and penniless in one's familiar island setting was dispiriting enough. To be equally destitute, and now homeless also, in Quebec or Montreal or Halifax was an even less attractive prospect. That was why dogs had to be used to hunt down dozens of reluctant emigrants; why some of those emigrants had to be forcibly conveyed to island ports like Lochmaddy and Lochboisdale; why John Gordon ordered the speedy removal of the crudely constructed tents and other makeshift shelters put up by Barra people whose stone-built houses had already been destroyed.

This was a time of horror, misery, despair and degradation. Something of its overwhelming impact can be discerned still in the remarks made by a Uist woman, Catherine MacPhee, whose personal recollections of Gordon's clearances were afterwards carefully recorded by Alasdair Carmichael, one of the several folklore collectors who, by the 1870s, were following in the pioneering footsteps of the Islay landlord's son, John Francis Campbell.

'Many a thing have I seen in my own day … many a thing, oh Mary Mother … I have seen the townships swept and the big holdings being made of them, the people being driven out of the countryside to the streets of Glasgow and to the wilds of Canada, such of them as did not die of hunger and plague and smallpox while going across the ocean. I have seen the women putting the children in the carts which were being sent from Benbecula and Iochdar to Lochboisdale, while their husbands lay bound in the pen and were weeping beside them, without power to give them a helping hand, though the women themselves were crying aloud and their little children wailing like to break their hearts. I have seen the big, strong men, the champions of the countryside, the stalwarts of the world, being bound on Lochboisdale quay and cast into the ship as would be done to a batch of horses or cattle in the boat, the bailiffs and the ground-officers and the constables and the policemen gathered behind them in pursuit of them. The God of Life and He only knows all the loathesome work of men on that day.'

Gaelic Scotland's age-old social order had been under mounting pressure since the overthrow of the last Lord of the Isles. Now, in the hundred years following Culloden, it had fallen apart everywhere. A people who, for very many centuries, had been so strongly identified with the Highlands and Islands were suddenly dispersed across the world to burgeoning industrial towns in more southerly regions of Britain, to Canada, the United States, Australia, New Zealand, South Africa and all the other faraway places to which so many Highlanders and Hebrideans fled in the era of clearance and eviction.

Those emigrants and their descendants were eventually to build new lives; lives in which, for all that Scots-Americans, Scots-Canadians and the like quickly became loyal citizens of their adopted countries, there was still a place – as in the case of Jim MacLeod with whom this book began – for a strong and lingering appreciation of what it had once meant to be a Scottish Highlander.

The steadily dwindling number of Gaels remaining in the Highlands and Islands in the later part of the nineteenth century, meanwhile, found it immensely difficult to come to terms with the implications of what had occurred. Nothing in their culture had prepared them for the circumstances in which they now found themselves. Their previously paternal chiefs, men to whom all precedent and practice demanded an unstinting loyalty, had been transformed into harshly exploitative landlords. Their language and traditions were under constant attack. Their grip upon the land itself was utterly precarious and insecure.

It was little wonder, then, that when John Murdoch returned to the Highlands and Islands in the 1870s to preach, as the former excise officer put it, the gospel of land reform, he found himself dealing with crofting communities which were wholly demoralised and dejected.

171

'We have to record the terrible fact,' Murdoch wrote at this time, 'that, from some cause or other, a craven, cowed, snivelling population has taken the place of the men of former days. In Lewis, in the Uists, in Barra, in Skye, in Islay, in Applecross and so forth, the great body of the people seem to be penetrated by fear. There is one great, dark cloud hanging over them in which there seem to be the terrible forms of devouring landlords, tormenting factors and ubiquitous ground-officers. People complain; but it is under their breaths and under such a feeling of depression that the complaint is never meant to reach the ear of landlord or factor. We ask for particulars, we take out a notebook to record the facts; but this strikes a deeper terror. "For any sake do not mention what I say to you," says the complainer. "Why?" we naturally ask. "Because the factor might blame me for it."'

When John Murdoch first came here to the Uists, he could not get an audience to attend his public meetings, so profound was people's apprehension that they might be evicted simply as a result of being seen in his company. But when staying, on one occasion, with his friend and fellow customs official, the folklorist Alexander Carmichael, who was living then at Creagorry in Benbecula, Murdoch happened to come upon a group of crofters attending to their sheep in the vicinity of Iochdar. 'They could not well run away from their work,' he afterwards recalled, 'and there they were at my disposal.'

There was much subsequent discussion between those South Uist crofters and the man their landlord called an agitator. From such small beginnings there developed the crofting protest movement of the 1880s. Crofters now organised themselves politically for the first time. The Highland Land League was formed and soon attracted a mass membership. Crofter MPs were elected to the House of Commons. Rent-strikes were initiated. Daring raids were mounted on the lands from which an earlier generation of crofters had been so brutally expelled.

Eventually, in the face of repeated actions of this sort, successive governments conceded much of what a newly self-confident generation of Scottish Highlanders were so vociferously demanding. Security of tenure was granted to crofters. Evictions were brought to an end. Here and there the clearances began to be reversed.

The South Uist and Benbecula which John Murdoch knew were islands characterised by enormous sheep farms; farms created by means of the evictions ordered by Clanranald and John Gordon; farms with names like Askernish, Bornish, Milton, Ormaclete, Drimisdale, Gerinish and Nunton. Every one of these had formerly been a crofting township. Now every one of them is a crofting township once again.

A LEWIS CROFTER AT THE CALLANISH STONES

On a quiet but colourless December morning, I head northwards on Benbecula's Atlantic coast, passing the once extensive farm of Nunton. Its sprawling nineteenth-century house and steadings, I notice, have a slightly crumbling, run-down air which contrasts, to their marked disadvantage, with the neat and trim appearance of the many modern bungalows on the surrounding crofts. Here, too, as in Strathnaver, a victory of a sort has finally been won; for had you come this way a hundred years ago, you would have been in no doubt as to the boot then being firmly on the other foot. In John Murdoch's day, and later, the Nunton farm complex – with its solidly constructed buildings, its two storeys, chimney stacks and slated roofs – would have compared extremely favourably with the low and tiny byres and blackhouses whose ruins can still be seen in the nearby crofting township of Aird.

At Aird, one of the few Benbecula settlements to have escaped being cleared, I call on Alasdair MacEachen, an energetic crofter who combines his agricultural activities – including his key role in the Benbecula branch of the Scottish Crofters Union – with his job as a local government environmental health officer.

Alasdair – translating from the Gaelic in which these things are usually stated – is the son of Donald Alexander, son of Alexander, son of Donald, son of Alexander, son of Eoghann, son of Iain Ban, son of Eoghann Mor of Drumandaraich.

The last named of these eight generations of MacEachens came to the islands in the seventeenth century, from his original home in Arisaig, to join the retinue of a Clanranald chief. And it is indicative of the sheer length of the MacEachen genealogy that it was this Eoghann Mor's grandson, another Eoghann, who represented the family at Culloden. Alasdair's father is recorded as saying that, although slightly wounded, his ancestor survived the battle. 'I have heard, however,' Donald Alexander MacEachen went on, 'that he was stripped even of his underclothes on Culloden field.' There followed 'two miserable years' in an English prison. 'Then Clanranald paid some money, a kind of ransom, to get him back here to Benbecula. And he got the land free of rent from Clanranald until the day of his death. That was the pension he got, the croft I reside on today.'

These words were taken down some twenty years ago and Donald Alexander MacEachen, great-great-great-great-grandson of Eoghann Mor of Drumandaraich, is now dead, his croft handed on to Alasdair, his son.

Outside it has begun to rain again. The autumn has been wet and stormy. Livestock markets have been bad. Lamb prices, at their lowest in real terms since the 1930s, are among the many casualties arising from the wider world's efforts to reform the European Community's policy on agriculture.

'There are times when I feel like leaving,' says Alasdair MacEachen. 'But I don't think I ever will. My people have put a lot into this piece of land. It would not be in me just to give it up.'

Not far from Alasdair MacEachen's croft at Aird, I walk along a beach of flat, grey stones and rippled, white shell-sand. The tide is out and the shore is littered with the ropelike stems of kelp cast up by recent gales. Looking down, I notice the faint scratchings left by feeding birds. The pungent scent of rotting seaweed comes and goes on the wind. Always there is the rushing, rising, falling sound of waves.

Travel due west from here and, having skirted Cape Farewell in Greenland, you would first encounter land, some three thousand miles distant, in Labrador. Follow that other Atlantic coast southwards, as the Vikings did a thousand years ago, and you would come, on the same latitude as the central part of France, to the St Lawrence estuary and Nova Scotia, the destination during the nineteenth century of so many people from these islands – some of my own ancestors among them.

My own connections with the Hebrides are centred mainly on Tiree. There, when five years old and visiting my father's relatives, I first experienced the sensation of walking barefoot on the sand beside an ocean which, instead of having hills beyond it in the manner of the sea lochs near to Duror, stretched on and on and on until it met the sky.

I do not remember a lot more about this first trip to an island; just the indelible impression made by the sheer vastness of the surrounding waters; just the equally memorable business of getting from the family croft down to the shore in a cart, or trap, drawn by a pony which was irritably lashing at the buzzing summer flies with its long tail.

But I have ever since liked every such locality, not least Tiree and the Uists. I like their enormous oceanic skies and what John Murdoch called their cloudscapes. I like their endless brackish creeks and pools and lochans. Most of all I like the smooth expanses of the machair and the way the clustered houses of the crofting townships – such as those I can see this morning across the bay at Iochdar – are so silhouetted on its otherwise flat and featureless horizons as to give each of these communities the appearance of a little fleet of ships far out to sea.

My people have lived in such places for generations; certainly since the birth, around 1760, of my great-great-great-great-grandfather, Donald MacDonald, and very probably for several centuries before that.

Donald's son John, my great-great-great-grandfather, it seems from the surviving evidence, was married in Tiree in 1808 to Mary MacPhail, the couple subsequently moving to South Uist where, in the 1840s and the 1850s, they were resident first at Stoneybridge and then at Ormiclete.

John and Mary MacDonald had a number of children. Lachlan, their eldest son, took on the tenancy of an inn at Gramisdale in Benbecula. Flora, one of Lachlan's sisters and my great-great-grandmother, meanwhile married a Benbecula man, Angus Martin, whose own father and mother, Ranald Martin and Marion MacDonald, appear to have been among the many South Uist and Benbecula people to leave for the Canadian colonies at the time of John Gordon's clearances.

Among Angus and Flora Martin's children was Mary Flora, my great-grandmother, who, in the early 1880s, left Uist to take a job as a domestic servant in Glasgow. There, in 1884, Mary Flora married a Tiree crofter, John MacPhail, with whom she now returned to the island which her grandparents had left more than fifty years before. The couple afterwards lived on John's croft at Cornaigmore where, of course, there was born their daughter, Flora, who was eventually to marry my gamekeeper grandfather, James Hunter.

No small part of this information has been passed on to me by John Bannerman, the Edinburgh University historian who gets a well-deserved mention in the Acknowledgments of this book and to whom I am related because, in 1855, Marion MacDonald, a sister of my great-great-grandmother, Flora MacDonald, married John's great-grandfather, George Bannerman, a South Uist miller.

This *Seoras a'Mhuilinn*, or George of the Mill, as he was known, was himself the son of a Sutherland-born soldier, also George Bannerman, who served, so his great-great-grandson tells me, with the British army during the Napoleonic Wars and whose own parents were very likely among the innumerable victims of the clearances arranged by Patrick Sellar and his associates.

There is, quite literally, no limit to the network of family linkages that can be constructed in this way; no end to those relationships which, in a manner reminiscent of the ceaselessly interwoven designs found in the pages of the Book of Kells, serve to establish some sort of tie between so many of the people, right across the world, who feel themselves to be, in some sense, Scottish Highlanders.

Begin, for instance, with my great-great-grandmother's brother, Lachlan MacDonald, he who kept the inn at Gramisdale where the causeway to Benbecula from North Uist now ends and where, in his day, there came ashore those travellers who had just made their way across the perilous tidal ford which then linked the two islands.

Lachlan Tirisdeach, Lachlan the Tireeman, as the innkeeper was called, died tragically: he appears to have been killed in a barn fire at Stoneybridge, South Uist, where he had earlier lived with his mother and father, my great-great-great-grandparents.

Lachlan's widow, Marion, or *Bean Ghramasdail*, the gudewife of Gramisdale, as she was known in Gaelic, was clearly a very forceful lady. At the age of sixty, with her three grown-up children, Mary, Archie Kenneth and John, she left Benbecula in 1884 for Canada where, a few years later, she remarried.

The bigger emigrant group of which this MacDonald family was a part had been sponsored, as it happens, by the notorious Colonel John Gordon's daughter, Lady Emily Gordon Cathcart, who, by this time, had inherited her father's estates in Barra, South Uist and Benbecula. Lady Emily's initiative, though it was not accompanied by evictions of the sort her father had organised, was nevertheless condemned bitterly by those Highland Land Leaguers and others who insisted that, instead of despatching her tenantry overseas, Lady Emily should have made room for them on the sheep farms which had resulted from the clearances of forty years before.

Bean Ghramasdail's son, Archie Kenneth, my Cornaigmore great-grand-mother's cousin, evidently shared something of the Land League attitude. Lady Emily's factor, he claimed in the course of a Gaelic song which he composed after his arrival in one of Canada's prairie provinces, 'cares nothing for the people in their distress. If Emily were to ask for their crucifixion, that beast would comply.'

His heart had been heavy, Archie Kenneth MacDonald declared, at the thought of leaving Benbecula. And the pro-emigration pamphlets which had been circulating in Uist prior to his departure – pamphlets, Archie Kenneth

ALASDAIR MACEACHAN, AIRD, BENBECULA

177

said, which 'ran down' the Scottish Highlands and 'extolled the virtues' of Manitoba – had proved a mere deception.

'When we arrived in the land of promise,' runs one of Archie Kenneth's verses, 'the frost was rock hard, more than twelve feet into the earth, and not even an ant could survive it. What a contrast to the joy of going barefoot to the moorland!'

But they survived, these people. Modern Canada, I know, contains a generous scattering of their grandchildren, their great-grandchildren and great-great-grandchildren – all of them descended, like me, from John MacDonald and Marion MacPhail who, nearly two hundred years ago now, came from Tiree to South Uist.

This December morning, walking on the Atlantic beaches of the island with which both myself and those Canadians are indissolubly linked, it occurs to me that, at some point in the future, I should like to undertake the sort of voyage of discovery made by Jim MacLeod of Coeur d'Alene – but to make that voyage, so to speak, in the opposite direction. My aim would be to find out more about what happened to those people from the Highlands and Islands who contributed so much to the development of North America.

In Harris I call on Bill and Chris Lawson who have turned their former schoolhouse home into one of Britain's most impressive genealogical research centres. Bill had helped me trace my South Uist and Benbecula ancestry. Now he shows me how he set about that particular job and the many other similar tasks he undertakes each year.

Row upon row of box files in Bill's office contain the better part of thirty thousand Western Isles family trees. Now his operation is being steadily expanded into North America; into Canada's Maritime Provinces, the eastern townships of Quebec, Ontario and all the other principal centres of nineteenth-century Hebridean settlement.

What began as Bill's hobby has become his full-time career and it is one he clearly enjoys. It is one that, equally obviously, gives tremendous satisfaction to his clients. 'When you can show a family from overseas the spot where their people used to live, they are naturally pleased,' Bill remarks. 'But when you can actually introduce them to relatives they didn't know they had, as quite often happens, then they really are delighted.'

Several generations on from the events which dispersed such a high propor-tion of the Highlands and Islands population, say Bill and Chris, echoing what I had heard earlier from Ann MacDonell in Spean Bridge, the sense of being connected with this place is still strong among the overseas descendants of the folk who went away.

Leaving Northton, where the Lawsons live, and driving towards Tarbert by way of Scarista and Horgabost on a road which overlooks still more dune-backed beaches and wide Atlantic bays, I think of a hillside cemetery I once took a stroll through on a hot and sunny summer's morning in Cape Breton Island, Nova Scotia. Each of this little graveyard's plain and simple headstones had the same inscription carved beneath common Hebridean names like MacAskill and MacLeod: 'Born Isle of Harris, Scotland'.

Those people grew up here; in townships looking out to Taransay and to the the high, distant tops of Husival, Leosaval, Cleisaval, Uisgnaval and the Clisham; in communities where the peat fires which burned continuously in every home, day after day, month after month, year after year, were indicative of a continuity so enduring as to be taken for granted by men and women whose entire upbringing had been such as to root them firmly in their own localities.

Here their parents had lived, and their grandparents, and the grandparents of their grandparents. Here the physical features of the place – its streams, its rocks, its knolls, its every little ridge and undulation – had their own distinctive and descriptive names which resonated through the ceaselessly repeated stories and traditions linking the present and the past, the living and the dead. Here there was a feeling of belonging.

Here, too, the land was good by Hebridean standards: green, grassy and productive. That was why it had been so thickly settled. That was why, in the early nineteenth century, it was cleared as so many other similar localities were cleared; its people being ordered out of their homes; their protests crushed by the troops and the police whom the landlords of that era could so readily call upon in times of trouble.

Some were sent to Harris's eastern coast where the ground was so infertile that such soil as there was had to be gathered together in heaps to provide sufficient depths for a potato patch. Others were sent across the ocean to the Cape Breton outpost where I was one day to see the place of their interment; to a country where these people, whose own island contained scarcely a single tree, had to break in new fields and farms from the forest which still surrounds the white-painted and timber-built homesteads of their modern successors.

What was it like, I wonder, to be evicted? To watch the fire put out in your grate? To see the roof stripped from your home? To turn your back on that home's surroundings? To trek with your weeping wife, your sobbing children and your few belongings to the port where the emigrant ships were waiting? To spend several weeks together in the stinking, airless, dark and battened-down holds of the ricketty vessel conveying you to a strange and frightening continent? To know you would never again set eyes on your own place?

Life in the Highlands and Islands had seldom been free of uncertainty. Viking raids, clan feuds and the eternal variability of the climate had seen to that. But nothing which had gone before – whether battle or massacre, storm or scarcity – had been anything like as cataclysmic in its impact as the clearances.

Nor was that impact a matter of physical suffering only. The extinguishing of community after community – in Strathnaver, Morvern, Uist, Harris and a hundred other places – snapped the myriad threads connecting people and locality; ripping apart the seamless web of shared experience which linked each generation with all those other generations which had gone before. This was what made the clearances so spiritually traumatic; this and the fact that many of the harshest expulsions and ejections were the work of men whose own antecedents were inextricably bound up with the society they now sought to destroy.

The nation's hoop is broken and scattered, said Black Elk of the similar dispersal of the Oglala Sioux. But he, the person whom his tribe regarded as their leader, had at least shared in his people's tragedy; he had not, in the manner of his Scottish Highland counterparts, helped bring that tragedy about.

Where once there had been the powerful feeling of cultural and social solidarity which one can discern still in the poetry composed at Ruairi Mor's Dunvegan and in those traditional tales which have a Lord of the Isles, for instance, swapping instantly improvised verses with a ragged boy who was herding cattle on a Barra beach, there was now only a profound sense of betrayal. Gaelic Scotland's chiefs had sold out their own folk.

When King George IV came to Edinburgh in 1822, a scattering of Highland gentlemen – in answer to a summons issued by Sir Walter Scott whose successful romanticisation of the clans was itself a pointer to the fact that those same clans no longer posed any sort of threat to the more businesslike world with which Scott himself was so strongly identified – got themselves up in kilts and tried to stake out their own special claim on Scottish sentiment. Partly they succeeded. Partly their successors are succeeding still; at those balls and games and gatherings, held now right across the world, which are our current versions of the Edinburgh pantomime of 1822.

But when I come across one of those characters, complete with tartan plaid and eagle feather bonnet, assuring a respectful audience, in the accents of the

BILL LAWSON, ISLE OF HARRIS

English upper class, that he is the chief of this clan or of that, I tend to dwell a little less on such a man's descent than on the extent to which his family may well owe its present privileged position to their systematic annihilation of so many of the things this self-same nincompoop is telling us he holds so very dear.

On a frosty winter's morning, with a fiery-looking sun just levering itself into view, I take the road that leads south out of Stornoway, the only settlement in all the Hebrides big enough to be described correctly as a town. My destination is a place called Calbost in the part of Lewis known as Pairc. With me is Angus MacLeod who was born there some three-quarters of a century ago.

Angus it was who took the lead in setting up the Scottish Crofters Union for which I worked for several years. And mostly when we meet our conversation has to do predominantly with crofting matters. Today, however, the talk has to do with Angus's latest enthusiasm: his typically unremitting effort, by means of a society called *Cuimhneachain nan Gasgaich*, Commemoration of our

181

Land League Heroes, to provide Lewis with a permanent memorial to the men and women who, in the 1880s, fought so hard for some restriction on the previously unlimited powers of landlords. That fight was especially fierce in Pairc where no fewer than three dozen different communities were cleared to make way for a single sheep farm.

Not far from Orinsay we stop and look out across Loch Shell to the Shiant Isles and to Skye beyond. Angus is speaking about the evictions which took place near here; about the various families who, driving their few cattle and carrying the irreplaceable roof timbers of their demolished houses, passed this spot on the morning of their removal. He names some of the individuals involved and some of their descendants. The grandfather of a man known well to Angus was among the people cleared that morning. And Angus's friend, as a small boy, thus heard the story of these evictions directly from one of their victims. Even in the 1990s, I think, only two human lifetimes separate us from the clearances.

Eventually, in November 1887, Lewis people rebelled against the treatment meted out to them. Much of Pairc was by then a deer forest, and in order to register the fact that their claim on the district was better than that of their landlord's deer, local crofters, many of them armed with rifles, invaded the sporting preserve and proceeded to kill several hundred stags and hinds.

Some of the lost lands were won back but by no means all. Deprived, therefore, of access to their previously vital hill pastures, Pairc's crofting families turned their attention to the sea, and fishing, not agriculture, became their economic mainstay. Soon there were hundreds of boats sailing out of the various tidal creeks and sea lochs on Pairc's north-eastern coast. Relative to what had gone immediately before, the place was now mildly prosperous. This prosperity, however, did not last.

We reach Calbost and come to Angus MacLeod's former home on a steep hillside high above a bay. There is no lack of houses here, but almost all are empty. When Angus was growing up in Calbost in the 1920s there were nearly two hundred people in the place. Now there is one man in his eighties.

Angus lists Pairc's other townships, working sunwise around the peninsula: Garyvard, Caversta, Cromore, Crobeg, Marvig, Gravir, Lemreway, Orinsay, Steimreway. Just before the First World War, Angus says, these villages had a total population of some 2,240. Now, in all of Pairc, there are fewer than 450 people. I ask why and Angus replies that the failure of the fishing industry is primarily to blame.

At Marvig we call on Duncan MacLennan who was one of the last of Lewis's old-style fishing skippers. Duncan shows us photographs of his successive boats – spanning, between them, the half-century between the 1930s and the 1980s. 'Greed and modern technology killed the fishing,' he says.

Duncan's own favoured technique was drift netting. Now recognised to be the near-perfect means of conserving the herring stocks on which the Hebridean fishing industry depended, because of the way in which a drift net takes only the more mature fish, drift netting was long scorned by Duncan MacLennan's mainland competitors.

'First they abandoned the drift net for the ring net,' Duncan explains. 'That brought them bigger catches. Then the ring net was given up for trawling. That brought bigger catches still. Then came purse seine nets which enclose an area of sea as big as Hampden Park and bring in herring by the ton.'

But just as the intensive sheep-farming methods introduced to the Highlands and Islands as a result of the clearances did immense damage to the land, depriving it of so much of its ecologically essential vegetation, so fishing of the type described by Duncan MacLennan wreaked environmental havoc out at sea. Seabirds of all kinds are scarcer than they used to be, Duncan comments. So are whales. So also, of course, are the fish on which these species – to say nothing of Pairc's human population – once relied.

Duncan MacLennan was forced to sell his boat when herring fishing was finally banned for several years in a belated and desperate attempt to protect endangered stocks which, a few years earlier, traditionalists like himself had been told were capable of being fished intensively for ever. The fact that he was right and that the fisheries experts were wrong is not much consolation. The latter, after all, are still holding down their well-paid jobs in distant cities. Duncan MacLennan's Gravir, meanwhile, gets a little bit less viable with every passing year.

For more than half a century now, Stornoway, where Angus MacLeod himself now lives, has offered better prospects than Pairc. Mainland Britain has usually appeared more attractive economically than Stornoway. North America, especially in the 1920s and again in the 1950s, has frequently seemed much more enticing still. And though Pairc – being an extreme example of processes which, in many other crofting localities, have recently begun to be reversed – ought not to be taken as typical of northern Scotland as a whole, it is difficult to come here without experiencing some very real foreboding for the Scottish Highland future.

Where once there were five schools, with more than 500 pupils between them, Angus tells me, there is now only one – attended by about two dozen children. And of all the children in Pairc – those attending the single local primary school, those making the sixty-mile round trip to the senior school in Stornoway and those who are still too small to be going to school at all – only eight can be described, in Angus MacLeod's opinion, as fluent Gaelic speakers.

One of the oldest Gaelic songs still sung in Scotland was inspired by the fate of those early-sixteenth-century rebels who tried, and failed, to restore the Lordship of the Isles. 'Today,' it runs, 'today, today has gone against us; today and yesterday and every day has gone against us.' It is a bleak thought, but an understandable one; a reasonable enough response to our protracted tally of disasters and defeats.

For a long, long time now the lights have been going out all over the Highlands and Islands; in Calbost in the twentieth century, in Rossal in the nineteenth. It has been no simple matter, when thus surrounded with the evidence of our own people's seemingly inexorable departure, to be confident about Scottish Highland prospects. It has been altogether more straightforward to give full rein to the pessimism which arises out of our own history and which has been so massively reinforced, in the course of the last two hundred years, by the peculiarly fatalistic brand of Presbyterian Protestantism to which so many Gaels began to turn for some sort of reassurance in the period of clearance and eviction.

There is absolutely nothing to be done, we think; nothing to be done about those Calbost houses emptying one by one; nothing to be done about the fact that here in Pairc, on an island where Gaelic is commonly reckoned to be in as vital a condition as anywhere in modern Scotland, the number of young people who are capable today of speaking their own language can be counted on the fingers of two hands.

It is all too easy for Scottish Highlanders to deal largely in despair; to wallow in the whisky-sodden melancholy of a Friday night in a Hebridean pub; to surrender to the gloomier doctrines handed out in church on Sunday morning; to conclude that, if every day has indeed gone against us, it was probably inevitable, or predestined, that it should; inevitable that Patrick Sellar should go free and prosper while James Stewart should be found guilty and hang; inevitable that our chiefs should become evicting landlords; inevitable that Culloden should be lost, MacColla defeated and the Lordship of the Isles destroyed; that Scotland's monarchs should have given up their Gaelic speech; that seventh-century Northumbrians should ultimately have preferred Canterbury to Iona.

In fact, there is nothing in our history to suggest that, in the course of all the centuries separating us from Colum Cille, events here in the Scottish Highlands have unfolded in accordance with some preordained pattern which has rendered human effort null and void. There is, however, a great deal of evidence to the effect that, whether accidentally or by design, our people have long been encouraged to undervalue their own merits; to set less and less store by their own traditions; to put aside those things which rendered them distinctive. And once we started giving even some small credence to those preachers and those teachers whose favourite theme was the innate worthlessness of our whole cultural inheritance, it became immensely difficult for us to respond constructively to the predicament in which we have found ourselves in modern times.

'The language and lore of the Highlanders being treated with despite,' John Murdoch said more than a hundred years ago, 'has tended to crush their self-respect and to repress that self-reliance without which no people can advance.'

About this, as about so many other matters, Murdoch was surely right. Foremost among the reasons for Scottish Highland quiescence in the face of forces which have come close to overwhelming us has been our very general acceptance, in the nineteenth century and subsequently, that practically everything about us – starting with that most fundamental human attribute, our language – could convincingly be deemed to be of practically no account. A people taught by almost all those in authority to take such a poor view of themselves is bound to be a people lacking in self-esteem, in dignity, in confidence, in enterprise, in energy, in resolution; in all those qualities, in short, which have their origins in a proper pride in one's own background.

That is why the most exciting and, in some respects, most unexpected occurrence in the Highlands and Islands this century has been the recent resurgence of interest in our history, our language and those various other aspects of our collective identity which have been for so long either denigrated or ignored. Only on the basis of a rediscovered sense of who and what we are, more and more Scottish Highlanders are beginning to believe, can we hope to provide ourselves at home with the opportunities so many of us have previously had to seek elsewhere.

It is in this sense that the overall regeneration of the Highlands and Islands economy, so long characterised by a chronic lack of dynamism, can be plausibly maintained to be impossible without a prior commitment to some degree of cultural renaissance – the latter being an arguably necessary prelude to the emergence of a more self-confident and outgoing attitude on the part of a people whose previous treatment, over several generations now, has been much more calculated to demoralise and depress than to enthuse and energise.

Such an overturning of longstanding approaches to the Scottish Highlands, especially on the part of those central government agencies which play so important a role in the region's affairs, will not be readily accomplished, of course. But the chances of a fresh start are nevertheless greater now than was the case even ten or twenty years ago; not least because of the extent to which those things which give both the Scottish Highlands and the Scottish Highlanders their distinctiveness are now appreciated by the wider world in ways they never were before.

While staying in the part of North America where this book began, I spent an hour or two with Lawrence Aripa whose business card, pinned still to my office wall in Skye, identifies him as a leading member of the Council of the Coeur d'Alene Tribe of Idaho. Lawrence told me of the attempts now being made to have his people's language introduced again to reservation children and I mentioned, in my turn, how in the Scottish Highlands and Islands today enormous efforts are being made to teach Gaelic in schools where it was once forbidden to use anything but English. Lawrence Aripa smiled at this and explained how, on his lakeside reservation, it has recently become the practice for a number of elderly people to be invited into their local classrooms with a view to inviting them to engage in conversation in this tongue that only they can speak with any confidence.

'One of these old men,' said Lawrence, 'when they brought him into the school and asked him what he could teach the kids in his own language, he just laughed and laughed and laughed. He had been punished in that same school, you see, for using the very words the teachers had become so anxious to hear from him. And I guess that just seemed to him to be so very funny.'

In another school and in another country, some five or six thousand miles distant from Lawrence Aripa's comfortably cluttered home, with its many mementoes of the endangered way of life this man is trying to preserve, my Strontian grandfather was similarly strapped for involuntarily breaking into the Gaelic which had been his only language until Victorian Scotland's educational authorities had decreed that he should give it up.

What was experienced by North America's native peoples was, of course, more devastating than what happened to Scottish Highlanders, but the two phenomena had much in common all the same. Both were among the consequences of the global expansion of what has come to be called western civilisation. Whether here in the Highlands and Islands or in the United States, that expansion took place at the expense of societies generally thought, by the nineteenth century's more Darwinian-inclined imperialists, to have lost out in the struggle for survival; societies ill-fitted, as Patrick Sellar commented repeatedly of the Strathnaver 'aborigines', for an age of trade and commerce.

'Understand me fully with reference to my affection for the land,' said Heinmot Tooyalaket of the Nez Percé, the Montana tribe into which there married the Gaelic-speaking fur trader from Torridon, Angus MacDonald. 'I never said the land was mine to do with as I chose. The one who has the right to dispose of it is the one who created it …. The country was made without lines of demarcation and it is no man's business to divide it.'

This was a philosophy as alien to those American interests which were to engineer Tooyalaket's destruction as were the very similar views of Scottish Highlanders to the men who undertook the clearances. As such the Nez Percé chieftain's thinking was contemptuously dismissed. But that, of course, was long before our steadily developing tendency to treat our natural surroundings as just so many more marketable commodities had resulted in the onset of the modern world's numerous environmental crises. It is not the least of history's many ironies that the commercially orientated social order which so spectacularly triumphed over both the Nez Percés and the Gaels is presently responding to these growing difficulties by trying to rehabilitate – in some small part at any rate – those traditional values which, in an earlier incarnation, that same social order emphatically scorned.

The way that nature was habitually regarded by the Gaels consequently appears much less old-fashioned now than it has done for several centuries; just as, at this time of mounting conservationist concern for the countryside, the part-time, unintensive character of crofting agriculture renders the crofter more attractive to the contemporary rural policy-maker than he or she ever seemed to the likes of Patrick Sellar.

Thus it has come about that the Uist machairs are today an officially designated Environmentally Sensitive Area where crofters are offered financial incentives to manage their land in accordance with those age-old practices which John Gordon, who so savagely depopulated this part of his estate, no doubt thought that he had brought completely to an end.

Although I deplore their tendency, on occasion, to describe as 'wilderness' those many Highlands and Islands localities which are, in fact, entirely artificial desolations created not so terribly long ago by human action of the sort which this book has described, I welcome very much the environmental lobby's current interest in the Scottish Highlands; for that interest, which is shared now by many millions worldwide, promises to safeguard much that I hold dear. It is my fervent hope that both my children – and their children's children's children – will, throughout their lives, be able, should they wish, to walk, as their ancestors have walked before them, among the Ariundle oak trees or on those flower-rich meadows that you find beside so many island shores.

It is my hope, too, that something else will survive; that there will not be broken, for a long time yet, the link forged, over the greater part now of two thousand years, between this place of ours and us, its people; that those coming generations will discover Scottish Highlanders still in the Scottish Highlands; that there will continue to be Gaelic sung and spoken among all those highly varied landscapes which the Gaels have made their own.

'Mhair i fos,' wrote Alasdair MacMhaighstir Alasdair, 'Is cha teid a gloir air chall, Dh'aindeoin go, Is mi-run mhoir nan Gall.' It endures yet, said Alasdair of his native speech and of the culture to which that speech gave access. And its glory shall not be lost despite the vilification and the great ill-will of those who are not Gaels.

There is less ill-will now than once there was. Today, for the first time in many centuries, our young people are being educated in our ancient language in Gaelic-medium playgroups, Gaelic-medium schools and a Gaelic-medium business college. Nor is this renewed interest in our Scottish Highland heritage confined entirely to the northern part of Scotland.

In the autumn of 1991, when this book was being written, it proved possible for a Scottish Highland rock band, Runrig, made up of men from Skye and Uist, to attract a capacity audience to a concert on the esplanade of Edinburgh Castle. And you would have very little sense of history if, on hearing Runrig's Gaelic music resound around the walls of the fortress where there took shape so many schemes inimical to Highlanders, you did not feel that, with this event, some sort of citadel had fallen; a citadel of the mind, maybe, but a citadel nevertheless. The language of the people who created Scotland, who gave the country both its name and its monarchy, but who have been relegated for so long to the nation's margins, this language is staging a definite revival.

In view of so much of what has gone before, it occurs to me, looking out of my Skye window at the mist and rain which are once again shrouding Bealach a'Chaol-reidh, it is desperately rash to be optimistic about the Scottish

Highlands. But their rashness, after all, was what the Romans and the Greeks liked best about the Celts. And we might as well be bold as be dejected.

In North Uist, towards the end of the many journeyings undertaken in connection with this book, I visited the Trumisgarry croft occupied by my friends, Ian and Joan MacDonald. It was evening and their children, Lillian, aged five, Keith, aged three, and Calum Archibald, still just six months, were being prepared for bed. English is seldom used among this crofting family. And as I listened to Lillian and Keith chattering in Gaelic to each other, and to their baby brother, it occurred to me that whatever else the future may or may not hold for Scottish Highlanders, one prediction can be made with confidence about this people who first settled here in Alba at the time of Colum Cille. For all that such a thing once seemed so desperately improbable, their language will at least survive into one more millennium. Alasdair MacMhaighstir Alasdair, I think, would have considered that accomplishment enough.

FURTHER READING

R. J. Adam, (ed.), *Papers on Sutherland Estate Management, 1802-1816*, Edinburgh 1972

John Bannerman, *Studies in the History of Dalriada*, Edinburgh 1974

John Bannerman, *The Beatons*, Edinburgh 1986

G. W. S. Barrow, *Robert Bruce*, London 1965

G. W. S. Barrow, *The Kingdom of the Scots*, London 1973

G. W. S. Barrow, *Kingship and Unity: Scotland, 1000-1306*, London 1981

Jeremy Black, *Culloden and the Forty-Five*, London 1990

J. M. Brown, (ed.), *Scottish Society in the Fifteenth Century*, London 1977

Alasdair Cameron, *Annals and Recollections of Sunart*, Oban 1961

J. L. Campbell, (ed.), *Highland Songs of the Forty-Five*, Edinburgh 1984

Seamus Carney, *The Killing of the Red Fox*, Moffat 1989

Nora Chadwick, *The Celts*, London 1971

Barbara E. Crawford, *Scandinavian Scotland*, Leicester 1987

Frank Delaney, *The Celts*, London 1986

T. M. Devine, *The Great Highland Famine*, Edinburgh 1988

Myles Dillon and Nora Chadwick, *The Celtic Realms*, London 1967

A. A. M. Duncan, *Scotland: The Making of the Kingdom*, Edinburgh 1975

Ronald Ferguson, *George MacLeod: Founder of the Iona Community*, London 1990

James Fergusson, *Argyll in the Forty-Five*, London 1951

Ian Finlay, *Columba*, London 1979

Philip Gaskell, *Morvern Transformed*, Cambridge 1968

Alexander Grant, *Independence and Nationhood: Scotland, 1306-1469*, London 1984

I. F. Grant, *The MacLeods*, Edinburgh 1981

I. F. Grant and Hugh Cheape, *Periods in Highland History*, London 1987

Ian Grimble, *The Trial of Patrick Sellar*, London 1962

Isabel Henderson, *The Picts*, London 1967

James Hunter, *The Making of the Crofting Community*, Edinburgh 1976

James Hunter, *For the People's Cause*, Edinburgh 1986

James Hunter, *The Claim of Crofting*, Edinburgh 1991

James Hunter and Cailean MacLean, *Skye: The Island*, Edinburgh 1986

Bruce Lenman, *The Jacobite Clans of the Great Glen*, London 1984

Michael Lynch, *Scotland: A New History*, London 1991

Kenneth Nicholls, *Gaelic and Gaelicised Ireland in the Middle Ages*, Dublin 1972

Ranald Nicholson, *Scotland: The Later Middle Ages*, Edinburgh 1989

E. Mairi MacArthur, *Iona: The Living Memory of a Crofting Community*, Edinburgh 1990

William MacArthur, *The Appin Murder*, London 1960

Calum MacLean, *The Highlands*, Edinburgh 1990

Loraine MacLean, (ed.), *The Middle Ages in the Highlands*, Inverness 1981

Loraine MacLean, (ed.), *The Seventeenth Century in the Highlands*, Inverness 1986

Gordon Menzies (ed.), *Who Are the Scots?*, London 1971

Willie Orr, *Deer Forests, Landlords and Crofters*, Edinburgh 1982

John Prebble, *Culloden*, London 1967

John Prebble, *The Highland Clearances*, London 1969

R. J. Ross and J. Hendry, (eds), *Sorley MacLean: Critical Essays*, Edinburgh 1986

Eric Richards, *A History of the Highland Clearances*, London 1982

Alfred P. Smyth, *Warlords and Holy Men: Scotland, AD 80-1000*, London 1984

K. A. Steer and John Bannerman, *Late Medieval Monumental Sculpture in the West Highlands*, Edinburgh 1977

David Stevenson, *Alasdair MacColla and the Highland Problem in the Seventeenth Century*, Edinburgh 1980

Derick Thomson, *An Introduction to Gaelic Poetry*, London 1974